GOLDEN AGE
2000

COMING OF THE PRINCE

DR. ONEAL CARMAN

Published by: **Gospel Gold Publications**- an outreach of the ministry of Dr. Oneal Carman

Printed by: Faith Printing Company
4210 Locust Hill Rd
Taylors, SC 29687-8911
803-895-3822

Editing and Layout by
Four Winds Publishing
P.O. Box 3102
LaGrange, Ga. 30241
706-884-5368

ISBN 1-885857-09-8

ALL CORRESPONDENCE SHOULD BE DIRECTED
TO

DR. ONEAL CARMAN
P.O. Box 232
ELIZABETHTOWN , KENTUCKY 42702

CONTENTS

Introduction   I

CONTENTS

SPECIAL MARKINGS

Throughout this book there are a number of special markings to bring the readers attention to the identified text.

> *Italic of script print is used to identify all Scriptures.*

📖   The open book is used to identify Key Scriptures.

Ψ   The candle holder is used when a list of topics or statements is made.

✟   Statements of spiritual importance.

①   A circled number found in text is a reference number to find the source of material in the bibliography.

Bold Print is used to draw attention to headers and important words or statements

It is the authors hope that these aids will increase your reading pleasure and understanding.

GOLDEN AGE 2000
THE COMING OF THE PRINCE

INTRODUCTION

Jesus, said we should *"watch"* for the signs of his coming in the final generation, *Mark. 13:34-37.*

Have you *watched* the rapid revolutionary changes of the world in 1991 ?

THE WHOLE FACE OF THE EARTH CHANGED.

New maps were made of the earth. The leaders of the world could not keep up with the multiple changes of 1991.

In the Hebrew Alphabet there are twenty-two letters. Each letter has a numerical value. The Apostle John in the Book of Revelation said, *"The **name** of the beast or the **number** of his name, represented by the number 666."* Rev.13:17. The Hebrew word *Shinah* is equal to the number 5752. The year 5752 on the Jewish calendar is 1991 on our calendar, and the word *Shinah* means,**"The Year of Change."**

WAS NOT 1991" *A YEAR OF CHANGE* " ?

Ψ   In one year the world witnessed the Persian Gulf War, indicative of the approaching *"Day of the Lord"*, *Isa 13:6.*

Ψ   The airlift of 18,000 Ethiopian Jews to Israel from Cush, or Ethiopia, on May 25, 1991, fulfilling *Isa. 11:11.*

Ψ   The agreement in Western Europe to remove the borders between the National States, to be a United States of Europe.

Ψ   The fast forward move to establish a one world order, Rev. 13 & 18.

Ψ   The fall of Communism and the dismantling of the Soviet Union.

Ψ   The convening of the Mid-East Peace Conference that will eventually lead to an Interim Agreement initiating the final seven years of this age.

Ψ   The final 7 year week of Dan. 9:27, Rev. 11:1-3. There will be no permanent peace in the region until the return of the Prince of Peace, *Isa. 9:6-7.*

   Then the Middle-East will be divided into three major parts and all the sons of Abraham will receive their fair share of land apportioned by the covenants God made with their ancestors.

Ψ   Revival - Harvest gained momentum with a renewed interest in Bible prophecy and the Second Coming of Jesus Christ.

Ψ   The search for the Messiah in Israel intensified, *Matt.23 : 37*

Ψ   As the time for the Birth of Christ Jesus approached, a phenomenon occurred. According to scientists there were two conjunctions of Jupiter and Venus in BC. 3, and a final conjunction of the two planets in BC. 2, making a triple conjunction of these stars.In ancient times,Jupiter was called the Star of David, and Venus the Morning Star. This triple conjunction occurred again as we entered the 1990's, an exact repeat. Twice in 1990, and the third conjunction in Sept.

II

1991. Jesus said, "there will be signs in the sun, moon and stars." Luke 21:25.

ALL OF THESE INCIDENTS,
COULD NOT BE CALLED,
MERE COINCIDENCE.

In the winter of 1991-92 a very unusual, deep snow covered Israel even into the Judean Desert. When the snow melted, a **new desert emerged**. A desert covered with, flowers, roses and fruit.

This was called " *a miracle* **" by CNN Headline News, on Sunday night, April 5, 1992.**

Gushing streams were also flowing in the desert. By 1988, when I was on an archeological expedition, there was a beautiful **grape vineyard** in the Valley of Achor, which is in the Judean Desert. *Hos. 2:15.*

📖 **Isa. 35:1-6,** *[1]"The wilderness and the solitary place shall be glad for them; and the desert shall rejoice, and blossom as the rose. [2]It shall blossom abundantly, and rejoice even with joy and singing: the glory of Lebanon shall be given unto it, the excellency of Carmel and Sharon, they shall see the glory of the Lord, and the excellency of our God. [3]Strengthen ye the weak hands, and confirm the feeble knees. [4]Say to them that are of a fearful heart, Be strong, fear not: behold, your God will come with vengeance, even God with a recompense;he will come and save you.* **[5]Then the eyes of the blind shall be opened, and the ears of the deaf shall be unstopped. [6]Then shall the lame man leap as a hart, and the tongue of the dumb sing: for the wilderness shall waters break out, and streams in the desert."**

III

WE HAVE A MORE SURE WORD OF PROPHECY.

📖 **2Pet. 1:19-21,** *19"We have also **a more sure word of Prophecy;** Where unto ye do well that ye take heed,*

as unto a light that shineth in a dark place, until the day dawn, and the day star arise in your hearts:20knowing this first, that no prophecy of the scripture is of any private interpretation. 21For the prophecy came not in old time by the will of man: but holy men of God spake as they were moved by the Holy Ghost."

More sure than even the disciple's eye witness accounts of our Lord's works and resurrection. That is how sure and accurate the scriptural prophecies are. **These prophecies are shining into a world of darkness, leading us on until the perfect day, the Day of the Lord.**

📖 **Prov, 4:18,** *"But the path of the just is as the shining light, that shineth more and more unto the perfect day."*

Bible prophecy is not of any private interpretation. It is open, clear and literal, not privately interpreted by individual spiritualizing and symbolizing until it becomes meaningless.

Bible prophecy maintains its own criterion.It means what it says, and it was divinely inspired. Thus a literal interpretation was utilized by the apostles and post-apostolic fathers well into the third century AD.

WHY A BOOK ON BIBLE PROPHECY?

IV

A knowledge of Bible prophecy is beneficial for preparing, faith-building, overcoming gloom, depression, and fear, and also for witnessing and teaching others.

Bible prophecy is conducive to building growth with rejoicing, and increasing incentive to work with greater vision in the *Kingdom of God.* It also serves as a warning to the unsaved while offering hope to them regarding the delights of the Kingdom in this world and in the world to come.

📖 **Heb. 9:28,** " *To them that look for him will he appear the second time without sin unto salvation."*

📖 **Prov. 29:18,** *"Where there is no vision, the people perish."*

📖 **Luke 19:12-13,** *Jesus said, "Occupy until I come."*

Bible prophecy is a superb faith builder in *St.John 14:29,* Jesus said, "And now I have told you before it comes to pass, that, when it is come to pass, ye might believe." Some Christians say they are not interested in Bible prophecy because there are so many conflicting opinions on the subject.

There are many interpretations, or conflicting opinions, on every subject in the Bible.

This is not a valid reason to shun the Bible, or abstain from the study of Bible Prophecy. This is why it is so important to FOLLOW BIBLICAL PROPHECY LITERALLY.

IT IS ALL IN THE BIBLE.

The solution is not abstaining from the Bible, but allowing the Bible to be its own interpreter. Many Christians say:

V

"I don't see the importance of Bible prophecy; I am not interested in what is going to be. I don't want to know the future. What more is there to say, after one has said, Jesus is coming back."

If you have this attitude, a vacuum can be created in which false conceptions can pour . Jesus said " take heed that no man deceive you, listen to my word " *Matt. 24:4.*

BECAUSE WE LACK INFORMATION, WE CAN BECOME INNOCENT TARGETS FOR DECEPTION.

Then the forces of new age, and humanism, paving the way for anti-Christ can move into this vacuum.
Many become the victims of deception, propaganda and infiltration.   Much propaganda, for example, is being diffused from the Middle-East today with Satan's attempt to obscure and abort Gods plan relative to that region in the world.

WE SHOULD BE INTERESTED IN ALL OF GOD'S WORD.

At least one-third of the Bible is directly related to prophecy. *Matt. 4:4,* "But He (Jesus) answered and said, It is written, man shall not live by bread alone, but by every word that proceedeth out of the mouth of God."
Bible prophecy not only involves the future, but it is being fulfilled now. It is happening today.   Prophecies uttered 2,500 to 2,700 years ago are today's headlines.

BIBLE PROPHECY IS NOT FRIGHTENING TO CHRISTIAN BELIEVERS. IT IS FULL OF HOPE, AND INCENTIVE FOR REJOICING AND VICTORY.

VI

The Apostle Paul continually related to the second coming of Jesus Christ as a future event. *1 Thess 3:13*, "To the end he may establish your hearts unblamable in holiness before God, even our Father, at the coming of our Lord Jesus Christ with all his saints." Paul refers to this event as **"That blessed hope."** *Tit. 2:13*, "Looking for that blessed hope, and the glorious appearing of the great God and our Savior Jesus Christ."

📖 **Isa.46:10,** *"Declaring the end from the beginning and from ancient times the things that are not yet done, saying, My counsel shall stand, and I will do all My pleasure."*

We have a sure word of prophecy. God has pleasure in bringing to fulfillment these things. We therefore should have pleasure in witnessing their fulfillment. Jesus enumerates many signs pointing to his return and the close of the age, and exhorts all to watch these signs.

📖 **Mark 13:35-37,** ³⁵*"Watch ye therefore: for ye know not when the master of the house cometh, at even, or at midnight, or at the cockcrowing, or in the morning:* ³⁶*Lest coming suddenly he find you sleeping.* ³⁷*And what I say unto you I say unto all,* **Watch.***"*

THESE ARE OUR CURRENT EVENTS.

Later on the Isle of Patmos, the Lord instructs the Church, "If therefore thou shalt not, watch, I will come on thee as a thief, and thou shalt not know what hour I will come upon thee," *Rev. 3:3*. In this same book of Revelation, the Lord says, **"Blessed is he that readeth, and they that hear the words of this prophecy, and keep those things which are written therein; for the time is a hand."**

When you see the words of this book being fulfilled , He is saying the time is at hand, *Rev. 1:3.*

THE BOOK OF REVELATION IS A BOOK OF VICTORY

The Book of Revelation is not a book of doom and gloom designed by God to depress and frighten the Christian believer. It is a book to warn the unbeliever, and to encourage, and uplift the believer. It is not a book of defeat, but a book of victory and triumph. *Rev. 17:14, "These shall make war with the Lamb, and the Lamb shall overcome them: for he is Lord of lords, and King of kings: and they that are with Him are called, and chosen, and faithful."*

📖 ***Rev. 19:7,*** *"Let us be glad and rejoice, and give honor to Him: for the marriage of the Lamb is come, and His bride hath made herself ready."*

📖 **Luke 21:28,** *"And when these things begin to come to pass, then look up, and lift up your heads; for your redemption draweth nigh."*

If the disciples were enthused about his coming 2,000 years ago, how much more should we be excited about His return now. One thing is certain; we are 2,000 years closer to His coming than the disciples were then. Mankind greatly needs the beacon light of prophecy today, for there is a divine purpose and blessing in Bible prophecy.

Humanity needs prophecy's guiding flashes of light and its inspiring hope and assurance to find the harbor of eternity.
Without the light of prophecy, the future is a vast unknown, a trackless desert, an uncharted sea.

VIII

Bible prophecy is God's index finger pointing the way for a world engulfed in growing confusion, disillusionment, and despair. Even the unbelievers and scoffers of the Lord's return are fulfilling Bible prophecy today.

📖 **2Pet. 3:3-4,** *[3]"Knowing this first, that there shall come in the last days scoffers, walking after their own lusts, [4]And saying, Where is the promise of His coming? for since the fathers fell asleep, all things continue as they were from the beginning of the creation."*

There is a vast reservoir of knowledge related to Bible prophecy: The destiny of Israel and Jerusalem, the Endtime Alignment of Nations, Endtime Revival Harvest, *Matt. 24:14,* The rapture of the saints, and The second coming of Christ Jesus, *Matt. 24:3,* The seventy weeks of Daniel *Dan. 9:24-27,* The Restitution of all things, *Acts 3:20-21.* The nature and characteristics of the millennial reign of Jesus, *Rev. 20:4.* The Heavenly City, *Rev. 21,* and much more.

FULFILLMENT OF PROPHECY TODAY

The elections of November,1992 have now put leaders at the national level, including a President that is now enacting policies and encouraging various elements to pursue legislation and local ordinances which are conducive to an immoral environment. Social and moral permissiveness will tend to increase and accelerate more rapidly as a result of the apathy of the Christian voters, willing to give up Christian values for false prosperity. We are about to reach the moral social acceptance level in proximity with ancient Sodom and Gomorrah.

As in the Laodician church, the end-time element of the world is composed of people lukewarm, complacent, apathetic, and given totally to the god of materialism.

IX

Practices which God calls sin, but which satan subterfuges with phrases such as contemporary thinking, modern expressive art, adult entertainment or an alternative life style. Yes satan has always had a alternative life style and Gods word condemns it as sin, blasphemy, adultery, homosexuality, abortion, and pornography.The devils alternative life style is darkness, *Rom.1:26-32. 2 Pet. 2:4-9, Luke 17:26-30, and 2 Tim. 3:1-5,13.*

Humanism embraces the so called new moral code today, which is actually as old as the devil and hatched in hell.

The Greek Epicureans condemned by the Apostle Paul, taught the same philosophy over 2000 years ago. The philosophies of no absolutes, no right no wrongs, just do whatever you feel to do. This doctrine today is expounded by the humanists,new agers, modernists, gay rights and liberals, *Acts 17:18.* There was also the Nicolaitans who even infiltrated the church, *Rev 2:14-16,20-22,* and were condemned by God.

The humanist tendency is to be self-sufficient in their own human strength instead of relying on the God of creation.

Christian people everywhere must stand up in our present day. Put on the whole armor of God. Stand up and speak out for Jesus and the truth. Shine a light on a society of darkness. Ban together as an army of love and truth. *Eph.6:11-13,* "put on the whole armor of God, that ye may be able to stand against the wiles of the devil. For we wrestle not against flesh and blood, but against principalities, against powers, against rulers of the darkness of this world, against spiritual wickedness in high places. Wherefore take unto you the whole armor of God , that ye may be able to withstand in the evil day, and having done all, to stand."

X

Lay the ax to the root of the tree's sin, *Matt.3:10.* For those who say Christians and Ministers should not get involved in social and political affairs, I say the **Bible itself is a compendium of the words of Gods people targeted against the moral and social evils of their respective time's.** The writers of the Bible spoke out on the issues of their day. We have that Constitutional progressive today, along with the clear mandate of God's Word. *Jonah 1:1-2 , "Now the word of the Lord came unto Jonah the son of Amittai, saying, Arise, go to Nineveh , that great city, and cry against it; for their wickedness is come up before me"* This was a message of national repentance.

We are not against the person who has the sin, but against the sin that has the person, just as we are against a cancer that has a person. Noah was a preacher of righteousness in his day we need to follow his example in this day.

The devil, author of all evil,creates confusion and distraction. All Christians should have one common denominator for united action, and that is to proclaim God's Word in contrast to social evils, both nationally and locally, espoused by liberals. Yet we should pray that God grant strength and wisdom, and reveal his will to those in authority, *1 Tim.2:1-3.* Read carefully chapter 13 Destiny of America.

The theme of this book is centered on the return of Jesus Christ,contemporary with the generation of Israel's National restoration. We will also discuss many signs, events and archaeological discoveries that revolve around this central theme.

WE DON'T HAVE TO BE AFRAID OF THE FUTURE, FOR GOD IS THE GOD OF THE FUTURE.

When Jesus returns, he will begin a golden reign of peace and justice. It will not be the end, but the beginning, of a time of better , not worse. I am not a pessimist looking at the turmoil of our present age as the death rattles of an old age, but rather as an optimist in Jesus Christ, I see it as the birth pains of a *New Golden Era*. We are living in the dawning of a new day. We begin on this road at Calvary, and someday this road will turn to Gold. We shall walk the golden streets of that Holy City in:

THE AGE OF GOLD

Oneal Carman

GENERATION
OF
THE GOLDEN JUBILEE

Chapter One

In the study of history and the classics, such as Greek and Roman literature, all ancient peoples looked backward to a **Golden Age** in their past. This is the primary distinction between Judaism and Hellenism. The Greeks and Romans envisioned the Golden Age at the *beginning* of their history. Israel saw the Golden Age at the *end* of their **history**, the Messianic age. Orthodox **Judaism still retains this hope.**

GATEWAY TO THE GOLDEN AGE

The Hebrew prophets told of *a generation* which would be a turning point in the course of history. A generation of song and poem, recited by sage and seer, *as a gateway to the Golden Age.* They viewed this generation as the dream of nations, the vestibule to a world of peace. It is the dawn of the Lord's day.

THE LORD WILL ASSEMBLE HIS PEOPLE

📖 **Ezek. 11:14-20** [14]*"Again the word of the Lord came unto me, saying,...* [16]*yet will I be to them as a little sanctuary in the countries where they shall come.* [17] *Therefore say, This saith the Lord God; I will even gather you from the people, and assemble you out of*

1

the countries where ye have been scattered, and **I will give you the land of Israel**. ....*19* And **I will give them one heart**, and **I will put a new spirit within you;**... *20* and **they shall be my people, and I will be their God"**

THIS GENERATION IS
SANCTIFIED AND BLESSED

📖 **Ezek. 36:28-31**, *28" I will be your* **God.** *29I will also* **save you from all your uncleannesses;** *and I will call for the corn, and will increase it, and lay no famine upon you.* *30And I will multiply the fruit of the tree, and the increase of the field, that ye shall receive no more reproach of famine among the heathen.31... ye* **remember** *your own* **evil ways**, *and your* **doings** *that were not good, and* **shall loathe yourselves** *in your own sight* **for** *your* **iniquities** *and for your* **abominations."**

A GLORIFIED GENERATION

📖 **Hag. 2:7**, *"I will* **shake** *all nations, and the desire of all nations shall come: and I will* **fill** *this house with* **glory**, *saith the Lord of Hosts."*

📖 **Isa. 11;6-11**, *6"The* **wolf** *also shall* **dwell with the lamb**,.... *7 And the* **cow** *and the* **bear shall feed**;... *9 They shall not hurt nor destroy in all my holy mountain: for* **the earth shall be full of the knowledge of the Lord**, *as the waters cover the sea. ...11 And it* *shall come to pass in that day, that the **Lord shall set his hand again the second time to recover the remnant of his people,...** "*

📖 **Ezek. 37:26-28,***The tabernacle will be returned. **The Lord's presence** will be with This Generation. He will make **His Abode** with them.*

📖 **Ezek.36:26-28, *Israel will walk in the Lords statutes.*** *The people will walk in **His Righteousness.***

A PEOPLE OF PRAISE

📖 **Ps. 102:16-22,***"When the Lord shall build up Zion, he shall ... 18 This shall be written for the **generation to come:** and the **people** which shall be **created shall praise the Lord....** 21 to declare the **name of the Lord in Zion,** and His praise in Jerusalem;..."*

HIS KINGDOM EXTENDED

📖**2Pet.1:19-21,Isa.60-:1-3,Dan.2:44,Luke21:27,32.**
*This Kingdom of God will be extended world-wide. His sure word of **Prophecy**; His **Glory**, His Kingdom of **Righteousness**, will be encompassed by His **Generation**.*

RETURN IN GLORY

3

📖 **Isa. 9:6-7, Dan. 7:27,** *This is the **generation** of our Lord's Return in Glory, to this earth.*

THIS LONG AWAITED GENERATION

It is true, people in every generation for two thousand years have thought Jesus would return in their own generation. But, our generation is **THE GENERATION,** being the only generation in two thousand years that has **witnessed** the phenomenal **restoration of Israel** and the **liberation of Old Jerusalem from Gentile dominion.** This was a prerequisite for;

THE GLORIOUS RETURN OF JESUS

📖 **Luke 21:24,27, and 32,** [24]*"And they shall fall by the edge of the sword, and shall be led away captive into all nations: and Jerusalem shall be trodden down of the Gentiles, until **the times of the Gentiles be fulfilled.*** [27] *And then shall **they see the Son of man coming** in a cloud with power and great glory.* [32] *Verily I say unto you, **This generation shall not pass away, till all be fulfilled."***

Combined with these major events are a multiplicity of other pertinent signs, all outlined by Jesus in the Olivet Discourse, *Matt.24, Luke 21,*to occur contemporaneously, **in one composite generation.** This is summed up by Major General Chaim Hertzog, former Israeli Ambassador to the

United Nations and President of Israel. In a 1977 interview with Hal Lindsey, he said,

> "EVERYWHERE YOU TURN IN ISRAEL TODAY,THE BIBLE IS COMING TO LIFE."

I'm not talking only about archeological discoveries, but about the international political scene as it affects us today. If you read the Biblical prophecies about Armageddon and the end days, and you look at the current realities in the world, and especially the Middle East, things certainly begin to look familiar. "The vast number of archeological discoveries in Israel have all tended to vindicate the pictures that are presented in the Bible. If therefore the Bible has been proven true concerning the past, we cannot look lightly at any prognostication it makes about the future." These are not the words of a preacher, but a world leader, and Jewish spokesman, Major General Hertzog.

Our generation in view of these signs is the most exciting chapter ever written in the saga of mankind. It is truly a privilege to be living today. Jesus asked these questions:

"WHO SHALL DECLARE MY GENERATION?"

" WHO WILL DECLARE MY RETURN?"

This is of great significance to the Lord God himself.

5

📖 **Isa. 53:8,** *"He was taken from prison and from judgment; and **who shall declare his generation?** for he was cut off out of the land of the living; for the transgression of my people was he stricken."* The generation of His return must be His generation or the **generation beginning His reign.**

📖 **Hos. 5:15,** *"I will go and **return to my place,** till they acknowledge their offense, and **seek my face:** in their affliction **they will seek me early."***

📖 **Hos. 6:2-3,** *"After two days will he revive us; in the third day **he will raise us up,** and **we shall live** in his sight. Then shall we know, **if we follow on to know the Lord:** his going forth is prepared as the morning; and **he shall come** unto us **as the rain, as the latter** and **former rain** unto the earth."*

📖 **2 Pet. 3:8** *"But, beloved, **be not ignorant** of this one thing, that one day is with the Lord as a **thousand years,** and a **thousand years as one day."***

📖 **Ps 90:4** *"**For a thousand years** in thy sight are but as yesterday when it is past, and as a watch in the night"*

📖 **Luke 21:32,** *"Verily I say unto you, This generation **shall not pass away, till all be fulfilled."***

This book will not set a date, day, hour or year for the return of Jesus, or for the rapture. *We will merely relate to **the signs** or characteristics and **the prophetic events*** *pointing to His appearing.* We will observe the signs of the season. We will document the factual, historical, prophetical, events which were to occur in our generation. It is my understanding of the scriptures that we can know the **"times and the seasons."**

TIMES AND SEASONS

📖 **1 Thess. 5:1-6,...** *"¹of the times and the seasons, brethren, ye have not need that I write unto you. ²For yourselves know perfectly that the day of the Lord so cometh as a thief in the night. ³For when they shall say, **Peace and Safety**; then sudden destruction cometh upon them, as travail upon a woman with child; and they shall not escape. ⁴But ye, brethren, are not in darkness, that that day should overtake you as a thief. ⁵Ye are all the children of light, and the children of the day: we are not of the night, nor of darkness. ⁶Therefore let us not sleep, as do others; but **let us watch and be sober."***

Here Paul addresses the question related to our knowledge of the Times and Seasons. *"Times"* here, translated from the Greek, is *Chronoi,* which means the times of prophetic events in chronological order.

"Seasons", or its Greek equivalent, *Kairoi,* relates to the characteristics of the events themselves. Paul is simply reminding the church he need not write to them regarding the times and seasons because they already know them.

They already knew the countdown of signs which would occur during the fig tree budding season, as depicted by Jesus Christ, Himself.

THERE IS A SEASON FOR THE BUDDING FIG TREE.

📖 **Luke 21:29-31,**"*And he spake to them a parable: **Behold the fig tree**, and **all the trees;**When they now shoot forth, ye see and **know of your** own selves that **summer** is now nigh at hand. So likewise ye, **when ye see these things come to pass, know ye that the Kingdom of God is nigh at hand.**"*

SUMMER

There is a season which closely follows the budding fig tree. It is called *"summer"*. Jesus had already told his disciples the signs of the times of Gentile fulfillment. Paul is not saying they cannot know or do not need to know the times and seasons. To the contrary, he is saying we need not write you because you already know these things. We must follow the text in the context of :

📖 **1 Thess. 5:1-6.** *Jesus will come as a thief in the night. **Sudden**, and **unexpected**.*

But, He is not coming to the church, because they are not "*of the night.*" They are watching the season, the budding fig tree, the approaching summer, the signs Jesus enumerated in *Mark 13* and concluded by saying , Watch

📖 **Mark 13:34-37** " *34For the Son of man is as a man taking a far journey, who left his house, and gave authority to his servants, and to every man is work, and commanded the porter to watch. 35Watch ye therefore: for ye know not when the master of the house cometh, at midnight, or at the cock crowing, or in the morning: 36Lest coming suddenly he find you sleeping. 37And what I say unto you I say unto all, Watch.* "

Watch what? I am in agreement with Hal Lindsey and many other prophecy scholars that we must continue to watch for the signs of that season as stated in Mr. Lindsey's book, The Rapture , chapter eight pages 117 and 118.

📖 **1 Thess. 5:1-6** NASB (translation),"*now as to the times and the epochs, brethren, you have **no need of anything** to be **written to you**. For you **yourselves know** full I tell that **the day of the Lord will come just like a thief in the night**. While they are saying, "Peace and safety!" Then **destruction will come** upon them **suddenly** like birth pangs upon a woman with child; and they shall not escape. But **you,** brethren, **are not in darkness**, that the day should overtake you like a thief, for **you are** all sons of the **light** and **sons of day.***"

We are sons of day not of night nor of darkness. So then,let us not sleep as others do, but let us be alert and sober. There are some who would refer to the scripture in :

📖 **Acts 1:6-8,** *"⁶When they therefore were come together, they asked of him, saying, **Lord, wilt thou** at this time **restore** again **the kingdom to Israel?** ⁷ And he said unto them, It is not for you to know the times or the seasons, which the Father hath put in his own power."* ⁸ *"But **ye shall receive power,** after that the Holy Ghost is come upon you: and ye **shall be witnesses unto me both in Jerusalem, and in all Judea,** and in Samaria, and unto the **uttermost parts of the earth."***

    The knowledge of the **times** and **seasons are in the Father's Power,**but you shall receive power after the Holy Ghost is come upon you.

This answers the textual question as to why Jesus followed His statement in verse seven with "it is",(present tense) not for you to know the times and seasons which the father has put in his own power, but here is a stipulation.

📖 **St. John 14:26** *"But the **Comforter,** which is the Holy Ghost, whom the Father will send in my name, he shall **teach** you **all things,** and **bring all things to your remembrance,** whatsoever I have said unto you."*
You have already learned of the characteristics of the season relevant to the Second Coming of Jesus. Our thesis in this book involves the prophetic signs in the generation and the season of our Lord's Return. We are not concerned with determining the day, hour or year of that blessed event.

10

We are observing however, the numerous prophetic events which have occurred and are mentioned throughout the Bible, all coming together, compiling incontrovertible Prima Facia evidence that we are presently living in the season and generation in which Jesus will come in glory.

It is interesting and somewhat of a curiosity to note that 1,948 years from Adam, Abraham was called out of Chaldea, and about 1948 Anno Domini (AD) Israel was reborn. In the center was Jesus Christ. Let us analyze :

THE SIGNS

📖 **Ps. 102:13-18** *"13Thou shalt arise, and have mercy upon Zion: for the time to favor her, yea, **the set time, is come.** 14For thy servants take pleasure in her stones, and favor the dust thereof. 15So the heathen shall fear the name of the Lord, and all the kings of the earth thy glory. 16When the Lord shall build up Zion, he shall appear in His glory.17He will regard the prayer of the destitute, and not despise their prayer. 18This shall be written for the generation to come: and the people which shall be created shall praise the Lord."*

Ψ 1. ZION

The Hebrew prophets applied the word *"Zion"* ⑦ to Israel and to Jerusalem specifically, because it is a mountain in Jerusalem.

📖 **Isa. 2:3,** *"And many people shall go and say,come ye, and let us go up to **the mountain of the lord,** to the* house of the God of Jacob; and he will teach us of his ways, and we will walk in his paths: for out of **Zion** shall go forth the law, and the word of **the Lord from Jerusalem.**"

📖 **Isa. 30:19,** *"For the **people shall dwell in Zion** at **Jerusalem:** thou shalt weep no more: he will be very gracious unto thee at the voice of thy cry; when he shall hear it , he will answer thee"*

📖 **Isa. 46:13,** *"I bring near my righteousness; it shall not be far off, and **my salvation shall not tarry**: and **I will place salvation in Zion** for Israel my glory"*

📖 **Isa. 51:16** *,"And I have put my words in thy mouth, and I have covered thee in the shadow of mine hand, that I may plant **the heavens**, and lay **the foundations** of the earth, and say unto **Zion, Thou art my people.**"*

Ψ 2. THE GENERATION TO COME

His throne is in Jerusalem. His throne is in Zion *Jer. 3:17, Ps. 2:6. In Ps. 102:16,* David said Zion would be built in the same generation when the Lord would appear in glory. In *Ps. 102 :18,* David said this shall be written for the Generation to come. In the Hebrew translation of the words *"Generation ② to come,"* is *Dor Achoron,* which in Hebrew means the last, or **hindmost generation.** I am a firm believer that the Hebrews understand their own

12

language. So I consulted them, and this is what they informed me is the meaning of the Generation to come in; *Ps. 102:18.* Generation here means a revolution of time in Hebrew. This is written for the generation in which our Lord returns in glory. *Ps. 2:6,* Not in suffering as a Lamb at Golgotha, but returning as the Lion of the Tribe of Judah, King of Kings at Zion. Doesn't it seem this is the same Generation of which Jesus Himself depicted in:

📖 **Luke 21:27-32** *"And then **shall they see** the Son of man coming in a cloud **with power and great glory.** Verily I say unto you, **This generation shall not pass away,** till all be fulfilled."*

Jesus is still referring to this generation as a future event.In the context of the parallel,or comparable accounts, of *Matt. 24 and Luke 21:24-32*, Jesus is referring to this generation as being at the expiration of Gentile dominion over Jerusalem. As the time of anti-Christ and the end of the world, in Greek, **"World"** aion or **age** as the time of the budding fig tree, or the rebirth of Israel, the time of harvest, and the time of His appearing in Glory, stated in *Luke 21: 27.* In *Luke 21:24,* **Jesus informs us of the termination of Gentile dominion over Jerusalem.**

📖 **Luke 21:29,** *"**Behold** the fig tree, and **all the trees;** when they now shoot forth, **ye see and know** of your own selves that **summer is now nigh at hand"***
So likewise ye, when ye see these things come to pass, know ye that the Kingdom of God is nigh at hand. Verily I

13

say unto you, this generation shall not pass away till all be fulfilled. Just as the budding of trees indicates summer is at hand, these signs appear just before the Kingdom of God supersedes the kingdoms of men. That is when the Times of the Gentiles are fulfilled. Christians are not Gentiles, but have been called out from among the Gentiles and will reign over the earth with Christ Jesus, *Acts 15:14*.

📖 **Rev. 20:4,**"*And I saw thrones, and they sat upon them, and judgment was given unto them: and I saw the souls of them that were beheaded for the witness of Jesus, and for the word of God, and which had not worshipped the beast, neither his image, neither had received his mark upon their foreheads, or in their hands; and **they lived and reigned with Christ a thousand years.***"

"Gentile" in Hebrew is *Goy* meaning ; heathen, foreign, or **outsider**. In Greek it is, *Ethnos,* meaning foreign, pagan, heathen or people. The Bible has much to say about the fig tree.

THE FIG TREE

📖 **Jer. 24:5,**"*Thus saith the Lord, the God of Israel; Like these **good figs,** so will I acknowledge them that are carried away captive of Judah, whom I have sent out of this place into the land of the Chaldeans for their good.*"

📖 **Hosea. 9:10,** "*I found Israel like grapes in the wilderness; I saw your fathers as the **first ripe in the fig tree** at her first time: but they went to Baalpeor, and*

14

separated themselves unto that shame; and their abominations were according as they loved"

📖 **Joel 1:7,** *"He hath laid my vine waste, and barked* **my** *fig tree: he hath made it clean bare, and cast it away; the branches thereof are made white"*

📖 **Matt.21:19-20,** *"19And when he saw a **fig tree** in the way, he came to it, and found nothing thereon, but leaves only, and said unto it, Let no fruit grow on thee henceforward forever. And presently **the fig tree withered** away. 20And when the disciples saw it, they marveled, saying, How soon is **the fig tree withered** away!"*

Israel withered, or became desolate, in the generation by 70 AD. Thus, the fig tree was the national symbol of Israel. Israel withered in 70 AD. Their house became desolate.

📖 **Matt. 23:37,"** *0, **Jerusalem,** Jerusalem, thou that **killest** the **prophets,** and stonest them which are sent unto thee, how often would **I have gathered thy children together,** even as a hen gathereth her chickens under her wings, and **ye would not!"***

♈ 3. RESTORATION OF THE FIG TREE

*Luke 21:29,*Jesus speaks of the restoration of the fig tree.③ In *Luke 13:6,*"He spake also this parable; A certain man had a fig tree planted in his vineyard; and he came and sought

15

fruit thereon, and found none." In *Matt. 24:32,* and *Luke 21:29,* Jesus did not say,learn a parable of a fig tree or fig trees, but **the** fig tree. **He is referring to one tree.** *Israel.* The first buds of the tree show the very beginning of its signs of life. The disciples ask Jesus what is the sign of your coming and the end of the age. *Matt. 24:3,* He gives them the one singular, major sign. The desolation and **restoration** of **Israel,**signaling the **Times of the Gentiles fulfillment.**

📖 **Luke 21:24,**"*And they shall fall by the edge of the sword, and shall be led away captive into all nations: and Jerusalem shall be trodden down of the Gentiles until the Times of the Gentiles be fulfilled."*

Ψ 4. THE BUDDING FIG TREE

The sign is the budding fig tree.④ This will enlighten you as to the approaching summer, or the summation of Gentile rule. The entire chapter of *Matt. 24,* and *Luke 21,* revolves around Israel.

📖 **Isa. 27:2-3,** *"In that day sing ye unto her, A vineyard of red wine. I the Lord do keep it; I will water it every moment: lest any hurt it, I will keep it night and day."*

Ψ 5. ISRAEL, THE FRUITFUL TREE

is still later, when **Israel** becomes a **fruitful tree**, not just a budding tree. The **revival,** or renaissance, of Israel becomes **complete.**⑤

16

📖 **Isa. 27:6,** *"He shall cause them that come of Jacob to take root: Israel shall blossom and bud, and fill the face of the world with fruit."*

Jesus entered Jerusalem on the first day of the week, which we call Palm Sunday.On the following day, he cursed the fig tree. His Olivet Discourse, *Matt. 24,* and *Luke 21,* occurred the next day. Jesus is illustrating to his disciples that the nation of **Israel would be withered and desolate and then would be resurrected or arise from the valley of dry bones, budding forth to life as the fig tree.** This was His answer to the disciple's question, "What is the most significant sign of thy coming and the end of the age?"

Ψ 6. NOW, RE-ESTABLISHMENT OF ISRAEL AS A NATION SETTING OFF THE COUNT DOWN

What would set off the final countdown in the final generation to His Coming? He is telling them: the re-establishment of Israel as a nation in the land of Palestine.⑥ *Matt. 24:3.*

Most Bible prophecy expositors believe the restoration of Israel was the major sign pointing to our Lord's Return.
The word **"summer"** comes from the word *sum*, because it is the **fulfillment of the annual cycle.** The evidence is inherent in the text of *Luke 21:31* itself, "So likewise ye, when ye see these things come to pass, know ye that the Kingdom of God is nigh at hand".

17

The context is the Times of the Gentiles Fulfillment is at the point when Jerusalem is no longer trod down under Gentile jurisdiction. This **point** was historically and dramatically, **reached** during the six days war of **1967.**

📖 **Luke 21:24,** *"And **they shall fall** by the edge of the sword, and shall be **led away captive** into all nations: and Jerusalem shall be trodden down of the Gentiles, **until the Times of the Gentiles be Fulfilled."**

The stipulation "until", at that point of Jerusalem no longer being trod down is the evidence of Gentile Fulfillment, in line with the context. The summer, or consummation of Gentile Kingdoms, **to be superseded by the Kingdom of God.**

📖 **Rev. 11:15,** *"And the seventh angel sounded; and there were great voices in heaven, saying, **The kingdoms of this world are become the kingdoms of our Lord, and of his Christ; and He shall reign for ever and ever."***

The answer to the disciple's question related to the end of the age,*Matt. 24:3.* Then what of all the trees alluded to, in *Luke 21:29 ?*

At about the time of Israel's declaration of independence as a sovereign nation in 1948, is it not true that the other nations subjected to colonial rule also attained their independence, as trees, budding to life and as sovereign states? States such as Jordan - 1946, Syria 1961, Egypt -

18

1951, etc. Nations in the Bible are in fact, symbolized by trees: Syria - the thorn bush or bramble, Egypt - flax or the reed, and Lebanon - the cedar. *Ezek. 29:6.*

📖 **Ezek. 17:3,** *"And say,Thus saith the Lord God; A great **eagle** with great wings, longwinged, full of feathers, which had divers colors, **came unto Lebanon, and took the highest branch of the cedar.**"*

In *Luke 21:32,* Jesus said, "This generation shall not pass away until all be fulfilled." The word ***generation*** here in Greek is translated, *Genea,* or Ghen-eh-ah meaning **age, span of time, revolution** or cycle. The transliteration back to Hebrew is *Dor Achoron,* meaning the last generation, or revolution of time. *Luke 21:32,* "Verily I say unto you, This generation shall not pass away, till all be fulfilled." Does "this generation" refer to the generation of the 20th century in which Israel was restored, or was it fulfilled in the generation prior to the destruction of Jerusalem, in 70 AD?

📖 **Rev. 11:15,** *"And the Lord shall be king over all the earth: in that day shall there be one Lord, and his name one."*

Did the fig tree, Israel, bud forth and did the kingdoms of this world become the Kingdoms of our Lord in 70 AD? The answer is evidently **no.** Nor did the great tribulation occur at that period in history. *Matt. 24:15-22, 29 and 30.* Nor was Zion built, *Ps. 102:16-18.* The center

19

and context of *Matt. 24, Mark 13,* and *Luke 21,* summarizing the Olivet Discourse, is the prophecy regarding Israel. Moses had predicted the Jewish nation would be destroyed and scattered to the ends of the earth, and would later return to their land and reform their nation.

📖 **Deut.28:63-68,** *"⁶³And **it shall come to pass,** that as the Lord rejoiced over you to do you good, and to multiply you; so the **Lord will** rejoice over you to **destroy you,** and to bring you to naught; and **ye shall be plucked from off the land** whither thou goest to possess it., ⁶⁴And **the Lord shall scatter thee** among all people, **from the one end of the earth even unto the other;** and there thou shalt serve other gods, which neither thou nor thy fathers have known, even wood and stone. ⁶⁵And among these nations shalt thou find no ease, **neither** shall the sole of **thy foot have rest:** but **the Lord shall give thee there a trembling heart, and failing of eyes, and sorrow of mind:** ⁶⁶And thy life shall hand in doubt before thee; and **thou shalt fear day** and **night,** and shalt have none assurance of thy life: ⁶⁷In the morning thou shalt say, Would God it were evening, at evening thou shalt say, Would God it were morning! for the **fear of thine heart** wherewith **thou shalt fear,** and for the sight of thine eyes which thou shalt see. ⁶⁸And the Lord shall bring thee into Egypt again with ships, by the way whereof I spake unto thee, **Thou shalt see it no more** again: and there ye **shall be sold unto your enemies** for bondsmen and bondwomen, **and no man shall buy you."***

Ψ 7 . THIS GENERATION WILL NOT PASS AWAY TILL ALL BE FULFILLED

Deut. 29, 30, and 31. The other prophets concurred, Ezekiel, Zechariah, Daniel, Micah, Amos, etc. Therefore, in the context of *Luke 21:24-32,* Jesus is focusing upon the generation that observes all these signs, or prophetic fulfillment's, especially the rebirth of Israel. This is the generation that will not pass away till all be fulfilled.

📖 *Luke 21:25-28, "25And there shall be **signs in the sun**, and in the **moon**, and in **the stars**; and upon the earth distress among the **nations**, with **perplexity**, the sea and the **waves roaring**, 26Men's hearts failing them for fear , and for looking after those things which are coming on the earth: for **the powers of heaven shall be shaken**. 27And then shall they see the **Son of Man coming** in a cloud with **power and great glory.** 28 And when these things begin to pass, then **look up,** and **lift up your heads,** for your **redemption draweth nigh.***

21

THE REBIRTH OF ISRAEL

Chapter Two

The Nation of Israel, separated from the nations, was composed of the twelve sons of Jacob, Grandson, or Seed of Abraham.

ABRAHAM

📖 **Num. 23:9,** *"For from the top of the rocks I see him, and from the hills I behold him: lo, the people shall dwell alone, and shall not be reckoned among the nations."*

Abraham worshipped and believed in the one true God, creator of all things, while all the nations round about worshipped a plurality of Gods.

📖 **Gen. 14:20-22,** *"20And blessed be the Most High God, which hath delivered thine enemies into thy hand. And he gave him tithes of all. 21And the king of Sodom said unto Abram, Give me the persons, and take the goods to thyself. 22And Abram said to the king of Sodom, I have lifted up mine hand unto the Lord, the Most High God, the possessor of heaven and earth."*

📖 **Gen. 11:31,** *"And Terah took Abram his son, and Lot, the son of Haran, his son's son, and Sarai his daughter in law, his son Abram's wife; and they went forth with them from Ur of the Chaldeans, to go into the land of Canaan; and they came unto Haran, and dwelt there."*

📖 **Gen. 12:1,** *"Now the Lord had said unto Abram, Get thee out of thy country, and from thy kindred, and from thy father's house, unto a land that I will shew thee:*

📖 **Gen. 21:12,**" *God spoke to Abraham,* **"In Isaac shall thy seed be called."**

INHERITANCE LINEAGE

The son of the bondwoman, **Ishmael, was not heir with Isaac**, the Son of Sarah.

📖 **Gen. 21:10,** " *Wherefore she said unto Abraham, Cast out this bondwoman and her son: for the son of this bondwoman shall not be heir with my son, even with Isaac. "*

The seed lineage of Isaac continued through Jacob and his twelve sons, with priests coming from Levi and the ruling tribe was Judah.

📖 **Gen. 28:4,13,**[4]*"And give thee the blessing of Abraham, to thee, and to thy seed with thee; that thou mayest inherit the land wherein thou art a stranger, which God gave unto Abraham.* [13] *behold, the Lord stood above it, and said, I am the Lord God of Abraham, thy Father, and the God of Isaac: the land whereon thou liest, to thee will I give it, and to thy seed;"*

GOD WILL ESTABLISH HIS KINGDOM

The Promise to scatter and return Israel to their original land constituted the Moabic Covenant,*Deut. 29:1, Deut-30:3,5,* and was reconfirmed in the Davidic Covenant.

📖 **2 Sam. 7:12,** "And when thy days be fulfilled, and thou shalt sleep with thy fathers, I will set up thy seed after thee, which shall proceed out of thy bowels, and **I will establish his Kingdom."**

📖 **Ps. 89:3-4,**"[3]I have made a covenant with my chosen, I have sworn unto David my servant, [4]Thy seed will I establish forever, and build up thy throne **to all generations. Selah.**"

Reconfirmed again in the New Testament, *Luke 21:24,* and *Rom.9:4.* The unconditional covenant of God given to Abraham regarding the land of Canaan, was an everlasting covenant, even to a thousand generations. Even if there were only 10 years to a generation, this would equal 10,000 years. It has only been 4,000 years since Abraham, *Ps. 105:6-11.*

Other promises and covenants of land were made appertaining to other sons and relatives of Abraham,who were the progenitors of other nations in the Middle-East. Aram - Syria, *Gen. 10:22-23, l Chron. 1:17.* Ammon and Moab-Jordan., *Jer. 49:1-4. Josh. 12:2,* "Sihon, king of the Amorites, who dwelt in Heshbon, and ruled from Aroer, which is upon the bank, of the river Arnon, and from the middle of the river, and from half Gilead, even unto the river Jabbok, which is the border of the children of Ammon." *Josh. 13:10,* "And all the cities of Sihon king of the Amorites, which reigned in Heshbon, unto the border of the children of Ammon."

📖 **2 Judges 10:9,** *"Moreover the children of Ammon passed over Jordan to fight also against Judah, and against Benjamin, and against the house of Ephraim; so that Israel was sore distressed."*

Ishmaal, son of Abraham and the bondwoman Hagar, and father of Arabs, spread across the Middle-East, Arabia, Egypt, the Sinai and also an admixture of the Palestinians, *Gen. 16, Gen. 25:12-18.* The ultimate land boundaries of Israel's inheritance are from the Red Sea to Hamoth in the north and from the Mediterranean Sea to the Euphrates River, *Gen. 15:18, Josh. 1:4, Ezek. 48:1,28.*

TRACING THE TITLE TO THE ABRAHAMIC LAND GRANT.

Original owner **God** - *Gen.1:1, Ps. 24:1, Ps. 89:11, Lev. 25.*

To **Abraham** *Gen. 12:1* - to **Isaac**, not Ishmael, father of Arabs - *Gen. 13:13-15. Gen. 16, Gen. 17:18,*"And Abraham said unto God, 0 that Ishmael might live before thee!" *Gen.25*:...Abraham gave all to Isaac Isaac to **Jacob**... *Gen.35:9-12*...God blessed Jacob   Thy name shall be Israel...... I give the land to the **12 sons of Jacob**......

Keturah - *Gen. 25:1-4,* second wife of Abraham and mother of the United Arab Emirates and Arabs in Arabia. Palestinians - mixture of Ishmaelites and Philistines. Tarshish and the Young Lion's - The United States, Canada, England; the colonies established by Phoenician traders, centered out of their great trading port of Tarshish, in Spain.

📖 **Ezek. 38:13***"Sheba, and Dedan, and the merchants of Tarshish, with all the young lions thereof, shall say unto thee, Art thou come to take a spoil? hast thou gathered thy company to take a prey? to carry away silver and gold, to take away cattle and goods, to take a great spoil?"*

EDOM OF ESAU - INTO WESTERN SAUDI ARABIA, INCLUDING MOUNT SEIR.

Gen. 25:30, "And **Esau** said to Jacob, Feed me, I pray thee, with that same red pottage; for I am faint: therefore was his name called **Edom**." *Gen. 32:3,* "And Jacob sent messengers before him to Esau his brother unto the land of

Seir, the country of Edom." *Num. 34:3,* "Then your south quarter shall be from the wilderness of Zin along by the coast of Edom, and your south border shall be the outmost coast of the salt sea eastward:" *Josh. 15:1,* "This then was the lot of the tribe of the children of Judah by their families; even to the border of Edom the wilderness of Zin southward was the uttermost part of the south coast."
1Kings 9:26, "And king Solomon made a navy of ships in Ezi-on-geber, which is beside Eloth, on the shore of the Red sea, in the land of Edom."

SHEBA AND DEDAN - PART OF SAUDI ARABIA *EZEK. 38:13*

Ezek. 27:22-23, "The merchants of Sheba and Raamah, they were thy merchants: they occupied in thy fairs with chief of all spices, and with all precious stones, and gold. Haran, and Canneh, and Eden, the merchants of Sheba, Asshur, and Chilmad, were thy merchants." *Gen. 10:7,* "And the sons of Cush; Seba, and Havilah, and Sabtah, and Raamah, and Sabteca.And the sons of Raamah; Sheba, and Dedan. *Gen. 25:3,* "And Jokshan begat **Sheba, and Dedan**. And the sons of Dedan were Asshurim, and Letushim, and Leummim." *Ps. 72:10,15,* "The kings of Tarshish and of the isles shall bring presents: the kings of Sheba and Seba shall offer gifts. And he shall live, and to him shall be given of the gold of Sheba: prayer also shall be made for him continually; and daily shall he be praised." *Isa. 60:6,* "The multitude of camels shall cover thee, the dromedaries of Midian and Ephah, all they from Sheba shall come: they shall bring gold and incense; and they shall shew forth the praises of the Lord."

Asshur - Assyria - Northern Iraq
Ezek. 27:23

📖 **Ezek 32:22**, "*Asshur is there and all her company: his graves are about him: all of them slain, fallen by the sword:*"

📖 **Num24:22**, "Nevertheless the Kenite shall be wasted, until Asshur shall carry thee away captive."

THE CHALDEANS

Chaldeans, Babylon, Southern Iraq in the Mesopotamian Valley.

📖 **Isa. 47:1,5**, "*[1]Come down, and sit in the dust, 0 virgin daughter of Babylon, sit on the ground: there is no throne, daughter of the Chaldeans, for thou shalt no more be called tender and delicate. [5]Sit thou silent, and get thee into darkness, 0 daughter of the Chaldeans: for thou shalt no more be called, the lady of kingdoms.*"

Ezek. 12:13, "My net also will I spread upon him, and he shall be taken in my snare: and I will bring him to Babylon to the land of the Chaldeans; yet shall he not see it, though he shall die there." *Gen. 24:10*, "And the servant took ten camels of the camels of his master, and departed; for all the goods of his master were in his hand: and he arose, and went to Mesopotamia, unto the city of Nahor."

THE GOLDEN AGE OF DAVID

Israel enjoyed her golden age under **King David and Solomon.**① Israel produced some of the world's greatest literature: the Mosaic Law; the history of great conquests; the inspired writings of the prophets; the proverbs; the poetical Songs of Solomon; and the Psalms of David. After the death of Solomon, the ten tribes of Israel began to practice of Idolatry, worshipping golden calves in emulation of Egypt.

JEROBOAM

📖 **1 Kings 11:31,35-37,** *"31And he said to **Jeroboam**, Take thee ten pieces: for thus saith the Lord, the God of Israel, Behold, I will rend the kingdom out of the hand of Solomon, and will give ten tribes to thee: 35But I will take the kingdom out of his son's hand, and **will give it unto thee, even ten tribes**. 36And **unto his son** will I give **one tribe**, that **David**, my servant, may have a light always before me in Jerusalem, the city which I have chosen to put my name there. 37And I will take thee, and thou shalt reign according to all that thy soul desireth, and shalt be king over Israel."*

They followed the leadership of Jeroboam and were taken into Assyrian captivity in 721 BC.

📖 **1Kings 12:28-30,** *28"Whereupon the **king** took counsel, and **made two calves of gold**, and said unto them, it is too much for you to go up to Jerusalem: behold thy gods,0 Israel, which brought thee up out of the land of Egypt. 29 And he set the one in Bethel, and the other put he in Dan. 30**And this thing became a sin:** for the people went to worship before the one, even unto Dan."*

📖 **2Kings 17:22-24,** *22"For the **children of Israel** walked in all **the sins of Jeroboam** which he did; they departed not from them; 23Until the Lord removed*

*Israel out of his sight, as he had said by all his servants the prophets. So was **Israel carried away out of their own land to Assyria** unto this day.* ^{24}*And the king of Assyria brought men from Babylon, and from Cuthah, and from Ava, and from Hamath, and from Sepharvaim, and placed them in the cities of Samaria instead of the children of Israel: and they possessed Samaria, and dwelt in the cities thereof."*

THE SOUTHERN KINGDOM

He left only the two tribes of Judah and Benjamin at Jerusalem as the Southern Kingdom of Israel. Still later Judah became corrupt and began to worship the idols of strange Gods. To preserve a seed lineage and to teach the nation a lesson, God allowed all except a remnant to be taken captive by Babylon.

JERUSALEM UNDER SIEGE

Babylon began the process of besieging Jerusalem, destroyed the temple and conquered Judah, subjecting it to Babylonian bondage.

📖 **2Kings 24:10,11,13,14**,^{10}*"At that time the servants of **Nebuchadnezzar**, king of Babylon, came up against **Jerusalem**, and the city was **besieged.**^{11}And Nebuchadnezzar king of Babylon, came against the city and his servants did besiege it. ^{13} And he **carried out** thence all **the treasures** of the house of the Lord, and in pieces all the vessels of gold which Solomon king of Israel had **made in the temple** of the Lord, as the Lord had said. ^{14} And he carried away **all Jerusalem**, and all the **princes**, and all the mighty **men of valor**, even **ten thousand captives**, and all the* *craftsmen and smiths; none remained, save the poorest sort of the people of the land."*

To fulfill the word of the Lord by the mouth of Jeremiah, until the land had enjoyed her Sabbaths: for as long as she lay desolate she kept Sabbath, to fulfill threescore and ten years.

📖 **Jer. 25:10-11,** *[10]"Moreover I will take from them the voice of mirth, and the voice of gladness, the voice of the bridegroom, and the voice of the bride, the sound of the millstones, and the light of the candle. [11]And this whole land shall be a desolation, and an astonishment; and these nations shall serve the king of Babylon seventy years.*

THE TIMES OF THE GENTILES

Babylon, under Nebuchadnezzar, was actually the first Gentile power to trod Jerusalem under foot, beginning the period called the "Times of the Gentiles."

📖 **Luke 21:24,** *"And they shall fall by the edge of the sword, and shall be led away captive into all nations: and Jerusalem shall be trodden down of the Gentiles, until the "Times of the Gentiles", be fulfilled."*

The Times of the Gentiles over Jerusalem is demonstrated by the metallic image in Nebuchadnezzar's dream, *Dan. 2:31-44.*

After the Babylonian captivity, both Israelites from the Assyrian subjugation and Judeans from Babylon returned to Israel and revolved around their great center at Jerusalem.

THE TEMPLE REBUILT

The temple and the city were rebuilt under the leadership of Ezra and Nehemiah.

📖 **Ezra 6:15-18,** *[15]And this house was finished on the third day of the month Adar, which was in the sixth year of the reign of Darius the king. [16]And the children of Israel, the priests, and the Levites, and the rest of the children of the captivity, kept the dedication of this house of God with joy, [17]And offered at the dedication of this house of God a hundred bullocks, two hundred rams, four hundred lambs; and for a sin offering for all Israel, twelve he goats, according to the number of the tribes of Israel.[18]And they set the priest in their divisions, and the Levites in their courses, for the service of God, which is at Jerusalem; as it is written in the book of Moses."*

📖 **Ezra 7:6,10,** *[6]"This Ezra went up from Babylon; and he was a ready scribe in the law of Moses, which the Lord God of Israel had given: and the king granted him all his request, according to the hand of the Lord his God upon him [10]For Ezra had prepared his heart to seek the law of the Lord, and do it, and teach in Israel statutes and judgments."*

RETURN TO THE LAW OF THE LORD

📖 **Ezra 6:3,** *"In the first year of **Cyrus, the king**, the same Cyrus, the king, made a decree concerning the house of God at Jerusalem, **Let the house be builded,**the place where **they offered sacrifices**, and let the foundations thereof be strongly laid; the height* thereof threescore cubits, and the breadth thereof three score cubits."

📖 **Neh. 8:1-2,** "[1]*And all the people gathered themselves together as one man into the street that was before the water gate;and they spake unto* **Ezra the scribe** *to bring the book of the law of Moses, which the Lord had commanded to Israel.* [2]*And* **Ezra the priest brought the law** *before the congregation both of men and women, and all that could hear with understanding, upon the first day of the seventh month."*

LET US RISE UP AND BUILD

📖 **Neh. 2:17-18,** [17]*"Then said I unto them, Ye see the distress that we are in, how Jerusalem lieth waste, and the gates thereof are burned with fir:* **come, and let us build up the wall of Jerusalem,** *that we be no more a reproach.* [18]*Then I told them of the hand of my God which was good upon me; as also the king's words that he had spoken unto me.So they strengthened their hands for this good work."*

📖 **Neh. 4:7,** *"But it came to pass, that when Sanballat, and Tobiah, and the Arabians, and the Ammonites, and the Ashdodites,* **heard that the walls of Jerusalem were made up,** *and that the breaches began to be stopped, then they were very wroth,"*

WHEN JESUS CAME TO EARTH

Israel was a tributary to the Roman Empire. *Luke 2:1,* "And it came to pass in those days, that there went out a decree from Caesar Augustus, that all the world should be taxed" Finally the Jews arose in revolt against Rome and they were crushed in 70 AD. The dispersion from 70 AD. is historically known as the second exile of Israel. The Roman army was well over a half million troops.

JERUSALEM DESTROYED

The city of Jerusalem was destroyed and trodden under the feet of the Romans. Then came the Bystantines, Moslems, the Mamelukes, the Crusaders, and the Ottoman Turks.

The long crusades with the callous warriors from Europe oppressed and persecuted the people of the Middle East. Thousands of Jews were murdered, tortured, and persecuted during the Spanish Inquisition of the 16th Century. The Prophet *Ezekiel, in Chapter 37,* informs us that:

JUDAH AND ISRAEL SHALL BE GATHERED

Judah and Israel, shall be gathered back into their land. after a world-wide dispersion. This is the same land of their origin, and they were to be one stick in the hand of the Lord, just as in the days of King David. The land of Israel, was woven by the Lord into the very heart of the Jew. The land is as much a part of Judaism as is the Torah, the Synagogue, or the language. The re-gathering of the scattered Jews among the nations was prophesied by Jesus in *,Luke 21:24,*beginning in 70 AD.

THE ZIONIST MOVEMENT

33

Israel passed into subjection from one kingdom to another from Babylon, to Persia, to Greece, and finally to Rome. Then Rome destroyed and scattered Israel. In 1897, a Jewish movement known as the Zionist movement was formed, simply for the purpose of restoring Palestine as a national homeland for the scattered Jews. Even Arab Kings agreed that the land should be a homeland for the Jews, under the terms of the Treaty of Constantinople,but the land of Palestine was possessed by the Turks.

DEFENDED AS WITH THE FLYING OF BIRDS

During World War I, Palestine was liberated from the Turks by the British under General Allenby. British airplanes flew over Jerusalem, and the Turks, having never seen airplanes, fled in fright, and the city was liberated without the firing of a shot in Dec. 1917. The Lord said he would defend Jerusalem as with the flying of birds.

📖 **Isa. 31:5,**"*As birds flying, so will the Lord of hosts defend Jerusalem; defending also he will deliver it; and passing over, he will preserve it.*" ②

Israel was then placed under the British Mandate by the League of Nations. It was still not an Independent State.

THE BALFOUR DOCTRINE OF GREAT BRITAIN

This doctrine declared Palestine a national homeland for the Jews in 1917. This was confirmed by the San Remo Treaty of 1922. On July 24, 1922, the Council of the League of Nations confirmed the mandate for Palestine to Great Britain. Under the terms of the mandate, the land of Palestine was to be a National Homeland for the Jews. The Arabs had been well represented at the peace conference.

34

King Feisal, the Emir of Saudi Arabia agreed to this arrangement. Feisal said that Zionist and Arab aims were not incompatible and he promised to support the Jewish demands at the peace conference.

On Jan. 3, 1919, Feisal signed an agreement with Dr. Weizmann which showed his complete accord with Zionism. Article IV of the agreement stated that all necessary measures shall be taken to encourage and stimulate immigration of Jews into Palestine, on a large scale.③ King Feisal wrote this letter to Felix Frankfurter, who later became a US. Supreme Court Justice.

Dear Mr. Frankfurter:

I want to take this opportunity of my first contact with American Zionists, to tell you that I have often been able to say to Dr. Weizmann in Arabia and Europe. We feel that the Arabs and Jews are cousins in race, suffering similar oppressions at the hands of powers stronger than themselves, and by a happy coincidence have been able to take the first step toward the attainment of their national ideals together. We Arabs, especially the educated among us, look with the deepest sympathy on the Zionist movement. Our deputation here in Paris is fully acquainted with the proposals submitted by the Zionist Organization to the Peace Conference, and we regard them as moderate and proper. We will do our best, in so far as we are concerned, to help them through; we will wish the Jews a most hearty welcome home. With the chiefs of your movement, especially with Dr. Weizmann, we have had, and continue to have, the closest relations. He has been a great helper of our cause, and I hope the Arabs may soon be in a position to make the Jews some return for their kindness. We are working together for a reformed and revived Near East, and our two movements complete one another. The Jewish movement is national and not imperialistic. Our movement is national and not imperialistic; and there is room in Syria for us both. Indeed, I think that neither can be a real success without the other. People less informed and less responsible than our leaders, ignoring the need for

35

cooperation of the Arabs and the Zionists, have been trying to exploit the local difference that must necessarily arise in Palestine in the early stages of our movements. Some of them have, I am afraid, misrepresented your aims to the Arab peasantry, and our aims to the Jewish peasantry, with the result that interested parties have been able to make capital out of what they call our differences. I wish to give you my firm conviction that these differences are not on questions of principle,but on matters of detail, such as must inevitably occur in every contact with neighboring peoples, and as are easily dissipated by mutual good will. Indeed, nearly all of them will disappear with fuller knowledge. I look forward, and my people with me look forward, to a future in which we will help you and you will help us, so that the countries in which we are mutually interested may once again take their place in the community of civilized peoples of the world.

Yours sincerely,
Feisal

" I WILL TAKE YOU FROM AMONG THE HEATHEN"

An estimated 6 million Jews were exterminated during World War II in Europe. This intensified the desire for the people of Israel to return to their own homeland. Ezekiel had prophesied that Israel would be scattered among the nations. Their dispersion was universal.

Ezek. 36:19 says,"and I scattered them among the heathen, and they were dispersed through the countries."Again Jesus mentions this still as a future event in *Luke 21:20-24*. *"For **I will take you from among the heathen,** and gather you out of all **countries,** and will bring you into your own land."* **Ezekiel predicts their return.**

📖 **Ezekiel 37:11-13,** *11"Then he said unto me, Son of Man, these bones are the whole house of Israel: behold, they say, Our bones are dried, and our hope is lost: we are cut off for our parts. 12Therefore prophesy and say unto them, Thus saith the Lord God; Behold, 0 my people, I will open your graves, and cause you to come up out of your graves, and **bring you into the land of Israel.** 13And ye shall know that I am the Lord, when I have opened your graves, 0 my people, and brought you up out of your graves,"*

ISRAEL GATHERED BACK

Our generation is the only generation in history in which Israel has been gathered back from the nations and returned to their own land. Notice Jesus and Ezekiel say, "Countries and Nations," in the plural, not singular. They are not referring to the Jewish exodus from Babylon, instead they are referring to a mass exodus from the nations or from the global dispersion from AD. 70, back into the original national boundaries of Israel.

AN IRREVOCABLE RESOLUTION.

On Nov. 29, 1947, the General Assembly of the UN. adopted a resolution calling for the establishment of a Jewish State in the land of Israel. This was as The Old Testament prophecies had predicted the Jews would return to the land just prior to the reign of Messiah.

As is stated in <u>Next Year Jerusalem</u> by Walter H. Price, "not by the wildest application of exegetical ingenuity or stretch of interpretative imagination can these bible predictions be said to have found fulfillment when Israel returned from the Babylonian exile in the 6th Century BC.

THE RESTORATION OF ISRAEL WAS TO BE FIRST NATURAL, THEN SPIRITUAL.

Ezek. 36:24-31 The full restoration of Israel was to occur just prior to the coming of Messiah.

📖 **Rom. 11:25-27,** [25]*"For I would not, brethren, that ye should be ignorant of this mystery, lest ye should be wise in your own conceits; that blindness in part is happened to Israel, **until the fullness of the Gentiles be come in.*** [26]*And so all Israel shall be saved: as it is written, There shall come out of Zion the **Deliverer,** and **shall turn away ungodliness** from Jacob:* [27]*For this is my covenant unto them, when I shall take away their sins."*

Zech. 8:2-3, "Thus saith the Lord of hosts; I was jealous for Zion with great jealousy, and I was jealous for her with great fury. Thus saith the Lord; I am returned unto Zion, and will dwell in the midst of Jerusalem: and Jerusalem shall be called a city of truth; and the mountain of the Lord of hosts the holy mountain." *Zech. 14:9,* "And the Lord shall be king over all the earth: in that day shall there be one Lord, and his name one."

📖 **Gen. 50:20-24,** [20]*"But as for you, ye thought evil against me; but God meant it unto good, to bring to pass, as it is this day, to save much people alive.* [21]*Now therefore fear ye not: I will nourish you, and your little ones. And **he comforted them, and spake kindly unto them.*** [22]*And Joseph dwelt in Egypt, he, and his father's house: and Joseph lived a hundred and ten years.* [23]*And Joseph saw Ephraim's children of the third generation: the children also of Machir, the son of Manasseh, were brought up upon Joseph's knees.*

*24And Joseph said unto his brethren, I die: and **God will surely visit you, and bring you out of this land unto the land which he sware to Abraham, to Isaac, and to Jacob.*"

EVERLASTING COVENANT

Moses reciting the Title Policy, *Ex. 32:13,* "Remember Abraham, Isaac, and Israel thy servants, to whom thou swarest by thine own self, and saidst unto them, I will multiply your seed as the stars of heaven, and all this land that I have spoken of till I give unto your seed, and they shall inherit it for ever."**This was an unconditional covenant, an everlasting covenant.** *Ps.105:6-11, Ps. 89:28-37, Ezek. 36:22.*

ISRAEL REGENERATED

The major friction in the Middle - East is rooted in theology between Islam and God's promise of land to Israel. The Theology of Real Estate. **Israel was born in one day, May 14, 1948 at midnight.** Israel as a nation was reborn or regenerated.

📖 **Matt. 19:28,** *"And Jesus said unto them, Verily I say unto you, That ye which have followed me, in **the regeneration** when the Son of man shall sit on the throne of his glory, ye also shall sit upon twelve thrones, judging the twelve tribes of Israel."*

39

ISRAEL'S TIMELY REGENERATION

Chapter Three

In *Matthew 24*, Jesus answers the disciple's question, "what shall be the **sign of thy coming**, and the end of the world?" ***"World"***, here in Greek , is *aion* or *age*. The one sign he explains is the rebirth of Israel. He is speaking here to Jewish people concerning the **desolation** and **restoration of Israel,** and Jerusalem the budding fig tree.

📖 **Matt.23:37-39,** "^{37}O, *Jerusalem, Jerusalem, thou that killest the prophets, and stonest them which are sent unto thee, how often would I have gathered thy children together, even as a hen gathereth her chickens under her wings, and ye would not! ^{38}Behold, your house is left unto you desolate. ^{39}For I say unto you, Ye shall not see me henceforth, till ye shall say, Blessed is He that cometh In the name of the Lord."*

📖 **Matt. 24:1,32,** "*^{1}And Jesus went out, and departed from the temple: and his disciples came to him for to show him the buildings of the temple. ^{32} Now learn a parable of the fig tree; When it's branch is yet tender, and putteth forth leaves, ye know that summer is near:"*

📖 **Luke 21:24,29-30,**^{24}"*And they shall fall by the edge of the sword, and shall be led away captive into all nations: and Jerusalem shall be trodden down of the Gentiles, until the times of the Gentiles be fulfilled. ^{29}And he spoke to them a parable; Behold the fig tree, and all the trees;^{30}When they now shoot forth, ye see and know of your own selves that summer is now nigh at hand".*

AS ISRAEL IS BROUGHT TO BIRTH, SHE WILL EXPERIENCE BIRTH PAINS

The birth of Israel was to be accompanied with birth pains as the Times of the Gentiles expire. A number system,

known as *Gematria* is built into Hebrew culture. There are twenty-two letters in the Hebrew Alphabet, or the Alephbeth. Each letter represents a number, or has a numerical value. Therefore, a word or a name is equal to a specific number.

THE NAME, THE NUMBER

📖 **Rev. 13:17-18,** *"[17]And that no man might buy or sell, save he that had the mark, or the name of the beast, or the number of his name. [18]Here is wisdom. Let him that hath understanding count the number of the beast: for it is the number of a man; and his number is Six hundred three score and six".*

HEBREW CLUES

📖 **2 Tim. 3:15,** *"And that from a child thou hast known the holy scriptures, which are able to make thee wise unto salvation through faith which is in Christ Jesus."*

The word *"scriptures"*, here when translated back into Greek is *Grammata*, in Hebrew it is *Gematria*. Jesus is building into his thoughts and words, Hebrew clues from the *Gamatria*, as to the timing of certain future events.

WHAT SHALL BE THE SIGN ?

Remember the disciples asked Jesus, "What shall be the sign of thy coming, and the end of the world?" *Luke 21*, gives the same set of answers. Luke is recording his version, or account of the Discourse of Jesus on the Mount of Olives. Did Jesus tell them what was the sign of His coming? Jesus

41

told them the **sign of Israel's rebirth, and the pains of the birth.**

📖 **Matt. 24:8,** *Jesus says, "All these are the beginning of sorrows."*

The word *"sorrows"* in Hebrew means **birth pains**, as it does also in Greek, *odin* , childbirth, pain, or travail. Israel was to have a rebirth, a rebudding of the fig tree.

THE LORD SET HIS HAND AGAIN, THE SECOND TIME TO RECOVER, THE REMNANT OF HIS PEOPLE

A regeneration , *Matt. 19:28,* a revival after 2 days, or two-thousand years.

📖 **Hos. 6:2,** *"After two days will he revive us: in the third day he will raise us up, and we shall live in his sight."*

A restoration again of the kingdom to Israel, still future after *Acts 1:6*. A restitution of all things pertaining to the Kingdom of Israel.

📖 **Acts 3:12,20-21,** *"12And when Peter saw it, he answered the people, Ye men of Israel, why marvel ye at this? Or why look ye so earnestly on us, **as though by our own power or holiness we had made this man to walk?** 20And he shall send Jesus Christ, who before was preached unto you: 21Whom the heaven must receive **until the times of restitution of all things,** which God hath spoken by the mouth of all his holy prophets since the world began."*

RAISE UP THE TABERNACLE OF DAVID

📖 **Amos 9:11,15,** *"11In that day will **I raise up the tabernacle of David** that is fallen, and close up the branches thereof, and **I will raise up His ruins**, and I will build it as in the days of old:15And I will plant them upon their land, and they shall no more be pulled up out of their land which I have given them, saith the Lord thy God."*

The word for *"rebirth"* in Hebrew is *Hay sheenit*. This word means to do over again, the second time around or **rebirth**.

Its Hebrew numerical value is 5708. **The year 5708 on the Jewish calendar is the same on our calendar as 1948.** What year was **Israel reborn** in, as a sovereign nation? **May 14, 1948 or 5708.**

Look at any Jewish calendar as a reference. Jesus said, "Jerusalem will be trampled or trodden underfoot by the Gentiles until the times of the Gentiles be fulfilled," *Luke 21:24*. He said not one stone of the Temple buildings will be left. *Matt. 24:1*, He said your house will be left desolate. The disciples then ask their first question,

"WHEN SHALL THESE THINGS BE? NOT WHAT,BUT WHEN. DID JESUS ANSWER THEM?

Did He tell them when Jerusalem would become a heap of ruins? Did he tell them when the temple would lie desolate? Did He speak the contents of *Matthew 24* and *Luke 21*, just to pass the time away? No! Jesus told them when Jerusalem would be destroyed. We know in accordance with history that Jerusalem was destroyed in 70 AD.① But their question was well in advance of that time. *Jesus said, "Jerusalem will be trodden underfoot by the Gentiles."* In

Hebrew, the statement, *"trodden underfoot"* is, *Yerushalem Tel,* meaning **"Jerusalem will become a heap."** A *Tel* in archeological terms is a manmade mound. It refers to armies of conquest reducing a city to rubble. The disciples of Jesus could have added up the numeric value of the words *Goim Tatel,* meaning a desolate heap, which has the numerical value *3830,* or when translated into the Gregorian calendar, *AD. 70.* The exact year in which Jerusalem was reduced to ruins.

JESUS SAID, "THIS GENERATION WILL NOT PASS AWAY UNTIL ALL THESE THINGS OCCUR." LUKE 21:32 OR MATT. 24:34

The word *"generation"* can be interpreted,**"this newborn one."** I believe Jesus was saying that "this newborn one" would survive to see all these other signs occur, wars, rumors of wars, earthquakes, famine, pestilence, and the universal preaching of the gospel.

In 1958 Israel minted a memorial coin to celebrate the tenth anniversary of the birth of Israel.

One side of the coin portrays a Roman soldier holding a sword over a woman who is on her knees. This symbolized the destruction of Jerusalem by Titus. The reverse side has an old man planting a fig tree and across from him is a woman holding up a baby in her arms to God. The baby is symbolic of the newborn Nation of Israel.②

A DOUBLE CHECK

Let's analyze and double check this system just to see if it works from another angle. Using the Hebrew number system applied to Gentile dates, since the Gentiles committed the act of surrounding Jerusalem. This approach is in accordance with Rabbinical principles of the language.

📖 **Luke 21:20,** *"When ye shall see Jerusalem compassed with armies, then know that the desolation thereof is nigh."*

"Compass", or to circle. *"Circle"*, in Hebrew, is

GIMEL LAMED   GIMEL   LAMED

3 $30\ 3\ 30$ $3 + 30 + 3 + 30 = 66$

In the exact year of *66 AD.*, Vespasian and the Roman armies first surrounded Jerusalem and **four years later the city was in rubble.**

GOD DID NOT FORGET JERUSALEM

📖 **Psalms 137:5,** *The Lord said, "If I forget thee, O Jerusalem, let my right hand forget her cunning."*

"If I forget thee" in Hebrew, is *Tishka Yimeni,* which has the Hebrew numerical value of *5728.* This on our calendar is *1967.* **Old Jerusalem was liberated in the six days war of 1967.**

OUR GENERATION

Since 1967, Jerusalem has been the Solo Rex Capital of a United Sovereign Israel, for the first time actually in 3,000 years since the reign of King Solomon, and **it occurred in our generation.**

In *Luke 21*, Jesus was speaking in the Hebrew language.③ His words echo through the stream of time to our very

45

generation. He is saying in Hebrew, the generation of *Sheenit,* and *Tishka Yimeni,* **the generation of the restoration of Israel and Jerusalem, in 1948 and 1967 shall not pass away till all be fulfilled.** This includes the fulfillment of *Luke 21:27 and 31.* During the Generation that began in **1948,** Jerusalem was restored in this same generation , **1967.**

THIS GENERATION IS STILL IN EXISTENCE. THIS GENERATION WILL NOT TERMINATE UNTIL ALL THINGS ARE FULFILLED.

But as to the hour, day, and even the year of His coming, we will just have to wait and see. **The season is here** and the **generation is definitely here.** We leave out the answer to the question, how long is a generation , 50, 70, or 80 years. It is not the purpose of this book to answer this question. We must also point out the Coming of the Lord could occur at any time during that generation before it transpires,because Jesus simply said, *"This generation shall not pass away until all be fulfilled."* This was the generation of which King David aspired. The generation in which Zion would be built. *Ps. 102:18* :

" THE GENERATION TO COME."

JERUSALEM THE GOLDEN

Chapter Four

The city of Jerusalem, nestled amidst the hills of Judea, located in the geographical center of the earth's mass, is a city of historical esteem. The word *"Jerusalem"*, means **shalom or peaceful.**In Hebrew ,*"Yeruwshalaim"*, founded peaceful, taken from **Twin Hills**, or **Jeru-Salem**. The word *"Salem"*, is also related to Jerusalem. *"Salem"* means **peace,**

📖 **Heb. 7:1,2,** "[1]*For this **Melchizedek**, King of the Most High God, who met Abraham returning from the slaughter of the kings, and blessed him. [2]To whom also Abraham gave a tenth part of all, first being by interpretation, King of righteousness, and after that also **King of Salem**, which is **King of Peace**."*

JERUSALEM,CITY OF PEACE

The word *"Salem"* is first mentioned in the <u>Bible</u> in the days of Abraham.*Genesis 14:18* states: "And Melchizedek, **King of Salem,** brought forth bread and wine: and he was priest of the Most High God" It is mentioned again as the site of the tabernacle, "In Salem also is his tabernacle, and his dwelling place in Zion," *Ps. 76:2.* **The location of the tabernacle is the temple mount, or Mount Moriah, in Jerusalem.**

📖 **2 Chron. 3:1,** *"Then Solomon began to build the **House of the Lord at Jerusalem in Mount Moriah**, where the Lord appeared unto David, his father, in the place that David had prepared in the threshing floor of Ornan,the Jebusite."*

The full term Jerusalem is first mentioned in:

📖 **Joshua 10:1,** *"Now it came to pass, when **Adonizedek, King of Jerusalem**, had heard how Joshua*

aken Ai, and had utterly destroyed it; as he had done to
Jericho and her king, so he had done to Ai and her
king; and how the inhabitants of Gibeon had made
peace with Israel and were among them."

JERUSALEM WAS CHOSEN BY GOD

As the location for the tabernacle, the ark of the covenant,
and the temple in the days of King David and Solomon, *1
Chron. 21:18, 28, 29.* The Jebusite dwelled at Jerusalem.

📖 **Josh.15:63,** *"As for the **Jebusites, the inhabitants of
Jerusalem,** the children of Judah could not drive them
out: but the Jebusites dwell with the children of Judah
at Jerusalem unto this day."*

SOLOMON BUILDS
THE HOUSE OF THE LORD

📖 **2 Chron. 3:1** *"Then **Solomon began to build the
house of the Lord** at Jerusalem in Mount Moriah,
where the Lord appeared unto David his father, in the
place that David had prepared in the threshing floor of
Ornan the Jebusite".*

The temple was built upon Mount Moriah at Jerusalem.

JERUSALEM WAS THE HEADQUARTERS OF
ISRAEL THROUGHOUT THE GOLDEN AGE.

📖 **Ps. 76:3,** *"There brake he the arrows of the bow, the
shield, and the sword, and the battle, Selah."*

📖 **2 Sam. 5:5,**" *In Hebron he reigned over Judah seven years and six months: and in Jerusalem he reigned thirty and three years over all Israel and Judah.* "
It was the civil, religious, and cultural center of Israel. According to *Judges 6:33*, "Then all the Midianites and the Amalekites and the children of the east were gathered together, and went over, and pitched in the valley of Jezreel."

📖 **2 Kings 10:11,***"So Jehu slew all that remained of the house of Ahab in Jezreel, and all his great men, and his kinsfolks, and his priests, until he left him none remaining."*

THE HISTORY OF JEWISH WARS①

Most of the wars were fought in the vicinity of Jerusalem, on the plains of Esdraelon, Jezrael Megiddo, and the valley of Jehoshophat.Future wars are mentioned in these areas.

📖 **Rev. 16:13-16,** *"13And I saw three unclean spirits like frogs come out of the mouth of the dragon, and out of the mouth of the beast, and out of the mouth of the false prophet.14For they are the spirits of devils, working miracles, which go forth unto the kings of the earth and of the whole world,* **to gather them to the battle of that great day of God Almighty.** *15Behold, I come as a thief. Blessed is he that watcheth, and keepeth his garments, lest he walk naked, and they see his shame. And he gathered them together into a place called in the Hebrew tongue,* **ARMAGEDDON.**" *Joel 3 and Zech. 14.*

CITY OF THE PROPHETS

Jerusalem was the city of the prophets.

📖 **Isa 1:1,** *"The vision of Isaiah, the son of Amoz, which he saw concerning Judah and Jerusalem in the days of Uzziah, Jotham, Ahaz, and Hezekilah, Kings of Judah."*

📖 **Ps. 137:5,** *" If I forget thee, O Jerusalem, let my right hand forget her cunning."*

Today the Dome of the Mosque stretches into the sky upon Mount Moriah, in Jerusalem. The scriptures testify that the Lord God Jehovah focused his attention upon Jerusalem and protected it.

📖 **Ps.135:21,** *"Blessed be the Lord out of Zion, which dwelleth at Jerusalem. Praise ye the Lord."*

The Lord gathered his people to the city to worship and to observe the major feasts of Israel: the Feast of Passover, *Luke 2:41-42*; Pentecost, *Acts 2:1*; and Tabernacles, *John7:37-39*. The beautiful dome of the temple could be seen for miles as one approached the golden city of Jerusalem. It was also the temple in Jerusalem to which Jonah looked, when he was delivered from the whale's belly.

📖 **Jonah 2:4,7,** [4]*"Then I said, I am cast out of thy sight, yet I will look again toward thy whole temple,"* [7]*"When my soul fainted within me, I remembered the Lord: and my prayer came in unto thee, into thine holy temple."*

DAVID LIBERATES JERUSALEM

King David liberated the city of Jerusalem, and 33 years later, Solomon, his son, began his reign of peace and built the temple. In our generation, Jerusalem was liberated in 1967. Every year for two thousand years, the Jewish people had said, "next year Jerusalem." 1967 was that next year. Thirty three years from 1967 would be the year 2,000 AD. This is just seed for thought. Sol-o-mon means son of man. Hos. 6:2-3.

WE DON'T KNOW THE DAY, OR THE HOUR, OR THE YEAR, BUT WE KNOW JESUS WILL COME IN THIS GENERATION.

The Kingdom will come in the generation of the budding fig tree. The summer season.

📖 **Luke 21:29-32,** *"29And he spake to them a parable; Behold the fig tree, and all the trees; 30When they now shoot forth, ye see and know of your own selves that summer is now nigh at hand. 31So like wise ye, when ye see these things come to pass know ye that the kingdom of God is nigh at hand. 32Verily I say unto you, this generation shall not pass away, till all be fulfilled."*

Israel will say, "After two days he will revive us; in the third day he will raise us up, and we shall live in his sight. His going forth is prepared as the morning, and he shall come unto us as the rain, as the latter and former rain unto the earth." Hos. 6:2-3.

Israel Eldad, renowned Israeli Historian, was quoted by Time magazine ,in 1967, as saying, "Just as Solomon built the temple in the same generation in which David liberated Jerusalem, so shall the temple be built and Messiah come in this same generation of Jerusalem's liberation in 1967."

JESUS CRIED OUT, " O, JERUSALEM , JERUSALEM"

📖 **Matt. 23:37-39,** *Overlooking the city, Jesus cried out, "37O, Jerusalem, Jerusalem, thou that killest the*

51

prophets and stonest them which are sent unto thee, how often would I have gathered thy children together,even as a hen gathereth her chickens under her wings, and ye would not! 38Behold, your house is left unto you desolate. 39For I say unto you, you shall not see me henceforth, till you shall say, blessed is he that cometh in the name of the Lord"

Forty years later, in 70 AD., this prophecy was fulfilled. Jerusalem and the temple buildings were destroyed, and the retainer wall around the Temple Mount was left standing. This is called the Western Wall, and Jews gather there from all over the world today to pray.

JERUSALEM SHALL BE TRODDEN DOWN OF THE GENTILES UNTIL THE TIMES OF THE GENTILES BE FULFILLED.

Jesus said Jerusalem shall be trodden down of the Gentiles, until the Times of the Gentiles be fulfilled.

📖 **Luke 21:24 says**, *" And they shall fall by the edge of the sword, and shall be led away captive into all nations: and **Jerusalem** shall be **trodden down** of the Gentiles, **until the Times of the Gentiles be fulfilled**."*

One of the most important and informative prophetic scriptures in the Bible is this statement of Jesus in *Luke 21:24*. This scripture is most pertinent to our present age. "Jerusalem shall be trodden down of the Gentiles, until the times of the Gentiles be fulfilled."

The word *"until"* is a very significant stipulation. The *"until"* signifies a certain given point at which Jerusalem will no longer be trodden down, or in subjugation to Gentile powers, and at that time, we will reach the fulfillment, or final generation of Gentile times. We can reverse this clause to read, ***"The Times of the Gentiles will be fulfilled when Jerusalem is no longer trodden under Gentile dominion".***

Jerusalem was to only be trodden down "until," (not forever) the fulfillment of the Gentile Age.

The Gentile Age is to be superseded by the Kingdom of God, under the peaceful auspices of King Jesus. "And they shall fall by the edge of the sword, and shall be led away captive into all nations: and Jerusalem shall be trodden down of the Gentiles, until the Times of the Gentiles be fulfilled." He spake to them a parable,

📖 **Luke 21:32** *"Behold the fig tree, and all the trees; Verily I say unto you, this generation shall not pass away, till all be fulfilled."*

THE SIX DAY WAR

In early 1967, Nasser, President of Egypt, sent Egyptian troops into the Sinai, and cut off the Gulf of Aqaba to Israel's shipping. This presented a direct threat to Israel's existence as a nation and to its security. Israel was outnumbered two and one-half to one in armament, and it was surrounded by over 100 million belligerent Arabs supported by the Soviet Union. This was like the story of David and Goliath, repeated on a national basis in modern times. But, in June of 1967, the Israeli Air Force made an early morning surprise attack against Egypt and the Sinai. As in days of old, Israel used surprise strategy. Israeli planes used diversionary tactic's by flying out over the Mediterranean as if on training maneuvers, then turned back and flew low over Egyptian airfields. Israeli jets flew over the Sinai as low as 30 feet from the ground to avoid Egyptian radar detection. They destroyed a large part of the Egyptian Air Force before the Egyptians could get their planes off the ground. In three days, a large majority of the air forces of Jordan, Egypt, Iraq, and Syria were destroyed. In six days time, Israel was victorious in her defense. In view of the odds, this would seem to be a miracle in our day, comparable to Israel's victories in the <u>Bible</u>. Israel had recaptured Sharm El Sheik, the Golan Heights, the Sinai, the Gaza Strip, the West Jordan Bank, and yes, the old city Jerusalem. O, Jerusalem!

Yes! For the first time since 70 AD, all of Jerusalem was now possessed by Israel. And for the first time since Nebuchadnezzer, Jerusalem was possessed by a sovereign, independent Israel: the capital of a United Israel for the first time since Solomon.

PROPHECY FULFILLED

The **prophecy of Jesus** was fulfilled. We have come to the Gentile's fulfillment: **the last generation**. The world was amazed. Jerusalem was remembered. The world said, "Better take a look at Bible prophecy again." "Must be something to this Israel-Jerusalem business". Yes, the city of history had spoke again, and is still speaking today. On that historic day of June 7, 1967, Premier Eskol stood in the city and proclaimed. "I send greetings of peace to our Jewish brethren wherever they be. Blessed be he who has kept us alive and enabled us to reach this hour."

A Sergeant Wassermann of Tiberius who, had led his men triumphantly into Jerusalem, was asked how he felt. He replied, "I, myself, feel that I have come home after 2,000 years." **People cried, rejoiced, danced in the streets, and sang „Jerusalem the Golden.** *"Jerusalem of Gold, of copper, and of light, for all thy songs I shall be thy lyre."* A soldier said, "I was glad when they said unto me," let us go unto the House of the Lord. Our feet shall stand within thy gates, oh, Jerusalem". In 1967, <u>Time</u> magazine said, "The repossession of Old Jerusalem by Israel was a fulfillment of Bible prophecy that had to occur before the Second Coming of Christ." When Jerusalem is restored, Jesus says, "There will be signs in the heavens and signs of decline in the Gentile world."

📖 **Ps. 122:2-3,** states, *"2Our feet shall stand within thy Gates, O Jerusalem. 3Jerusalem is built as a city that is compact together."*

Jerusalem was a divided city until 1967. Old or East Jerusalem was still subject to Gentile, or Jordanian rule. Western or modern Jerusalem had been built up by the new state of Israel. In *Ps. 122:3*, the word ***"builded"*** here in Hebrew is *Banah* or *Bow*,now meaning **repair**, or to set up, and the word ***"compact"***, here in Hebrew is *Chabar* or *Khowbor* meaning **to couple together** or to join together. In 1967, when old or east Jerusalem was liberated from Jordan, it was joined together, or **coupled** with west Jerusalem and to Israel.

FIVE STAGES
IN THE GROWTH OF ISRAEL

Chapter Five

The Bible was written from a background of Hebrew culture. It was written in the Hebrew language, by Hebrew writers. The word "*generation*" in Greek implies either a period of time or a person, from the Greek word *Genea*. The word "*regeneration*", from *Matt. 19:28,* in the Greek translation, is *Paliggenesia,* or Pal-ing-ghen-es-ee-ah, meaning **rebirth or restoration.** The word "*Generation*" then applies to the birth of a person, or a new born one.

REGENERATION,REBIRTH OR RESTORATION

In *Matt. 19:28,* Jesus said, "Verily I say unto you that ye which have followed me, in the **regeneration** or **rebirth** when the son of man shall sit on the throne of His Glory, ye also shall sit upon twelve thrones, judging the twelve tribes of Israel."

REGENERATION OF WHAT ?

Jesus here is speaking to the twelve disciples. In the text of the verse, he is saying to those who have followed Him **"now"** in the regeneration or rebirth of Israel, *Hos. 6:2, Ezek. 37.* He will return in glory and sit on the Throne of His Glory in Jerusalem. He did not do that 2,000 years ago. For that reason the disciples themselves were disappointed. But, when He returns to a **restored Israel,** this will be accomplished.

📖 **Jer. 3:17,** *"At that time they shall call Jerusalem the throne of the Lord; and all the nations shall be gathered unto it, to the name of the Lord, to Jerusalem:*

neither shall they walk any more after imagination of their evil heart."

📖 **Zech. 14:9,** *"And the Lord shall be king over all the earth: in that day shall there be one Lord, and His Name One."*

📖 **Luke 21:27,31,**[27]*"And then shall they see the Son of man coming in a cloud with power and great glory.*[31]*"So likewise ye, when ye see these things come to pass, know ye that the kingdom of God is nigh at hand."*

Then the twelve apostles will constitute the Supreme Court of Israel during the Messianic Age. They will be Judges upon twelve thrones. Therefore, the regeneration, or rebirth of Israel, is as the **birth, or rebirth** of a person. **A Generation.**

FIVE MAJOR STAGES IN A JEWISH GENERATION

There are five major stages in a Jewish Generation. The first stage is birth and the early days. The early days are the most critical in the life of the child. Circumcision occurs on the eight day from birth. So it has been with the generation or regeneration of Israel. Israel was born May 14, 1948.

First, The *early life* of a new born Jewish person, which includes the critical stage of circumcision. *Gen. 21:4,* "And Abraham circumcised his son Isaac being eight days old, as God had commanded him." *Second, Bar Mitzvah,* when the young Jew is in his thirteenth year, becomes an equal member of the family. *Third,* In the *20th year* when a young man is numbered for war.

📖 **Num.1:3,** *"From twenty years old and upward, all that are able to go forth to war in Israel: thou and Aaron shall number them by their armies."*

Fourth, at *age 30* when the young Levitical man is consecrated for the priesthood.*Num. 4:3*, "From thirty years old and upward even until fifty years old, all that enter into the host, to do the work in the tabernacle of the congregation." **Fifth**, At *age 50* when the priest or public servant retired from public life. A **Jubilee** year was also the **50th year**. *Num.4:3 Lev. 25.*

Since the individual Jewish newborn, or generation, is the micro-personification of Israel, the same five major events would occur historically in the life, or generation, of the new-born nation. Has that historical pattern of Israel matched the life of the individual Jew? Let us all look at history together.

HISTORICAL PATTERNS

First, *Israel was born* May 14, 1948. Within eight days Arabs attacked Israel cutting Israel off , Israel's 8th day *circumcision* , the Egyptian air force bombed Tel Aviv. The Egyptian army also crossed Israel's border. Then, the armies of Syria and Lebanon invaded Israel from the north, while Iraqis came in from the east. The trans-Jordan regions were already in Israel. This force was soon joined by Saudi Arabia. When Israel became a state, British Field Marshall Montgomery wrote that it would take the Arabs 8-10 days to drive the Jews from the land into the sea. This fulfilled the national ritual of circumcision for Israel as a nation. Many thought Israel would not survive these early days, even after they became a nation. But again the sons of Jacob were not consumed. *Mal. 3:6*, "For I am the Lord, I change not; therefore ye sons of Jacob are not consumed."

Secondly, in 1960, Israel captured Adolf Eichman, Nazi Jewish exterminator during the Holocaust. He was convicted and executed by Israel. The United Nations condemned Israel. Israeli Prime Minister David Ben Gurion made a speech in which he countered the condemnation on the basis of world failure to recognize Israel's plight.

Golda Meir, the Israeli ambassador to the UN., made an impassioned speech to the UN. General Assembly in which she reminded them that you cannot condemn that which is not recognized to exist. From that time, on Israel was recognized as an *equal nation in the world family of nations.*Russia made a motion to set Israel at the table of nations. From this time on Israel was recognized as a member of the family of nations. **This was Israel's Bar Mitzvah as a nation.** This was 1960/61, Israel's 13th year. *Bar Mitzvah year.* 1948 + 12 = 1960, or the 13th year 1961.

Thirdly, when Israel was in their *20th year,* the very significant **Six Days War** was fought which liberated Jerusalem.

Fourth, When Israel was exactly *30 years old* in 1978, the school of the **Cohenite Priesthood** was established to prepare the tabernacle priesthood of Israel. The school was begun by Rabbi Motti Hacohen. This is written in the book Prophecy 2,000 by Dr. David A. Lewis. Dr. Lewis reports, "arrangements were made to use the Hall first, in the Moslem section of Jerusalem during Passover, 1978."

Fifth, *50 years* expires in 1997. *The Jubilee year* precedes this. At about this time a great change will have been made. That is not to say it will be the Rapture, or the Coming of the Lord, but the **Jubilee Restoration of Israel** will have been accomplished. This is also not to say that 50 years is the expiration of this generation, anymore than 50 years is the end of a Jewish lifetime. You may go as high as 70-80 years to a generation. In *Ps 90:10,* this corresponds to David's scale, "The days of our years are threescore years and ten; and if by reason of strength they be fourscore years, yet is their strength labor and sorrow; for it is soon cut off, and we fly away." But after 50 years a new High Priest took charge. Jesus is our High Priest, and he is going to reign at a new beginning.

Jesus can return anytime during the generation. But, these analogies serve as milestones, or special events of our time. This is certainly seed for thought, and not intended in a dogmatic or doctrinal sense.

THE GOLDEN JUBILEE
RESTITUTION OF ALL THINGS

Chapter Six

After Jesus resurrected, the disciples inquired of Jesus, "Will you at this time restore again the Kingdom to Israel?" *Acts 1:6.* The question was not "**if**," but "**when**." This question was firmly predicated upon the projection of scriptures related to the future restoration of Israel as a Kingdom. For example, *Ezek. 37,* and *Amos 9:11.* The Apostle Peter later addresses the proposition of the restoration of Israel in *Acts 3:20-21.* He is directing his remarks to Israel, because he says,"ye men of Israel;" in *Acts 3 verse 12.* He explains in *Acts 3:20-21,* that Jesus Christ will be sent in the future. *"The same Jesus, which before was preached unto them. Whom the heavens must receive until the times of restitution of all things, which God hath spoken by the mouth of all his holy prophets since the world began."* *Luke 24:51,* states Jesus was parted from the disciples, and was carried up into heaven. This scripture,in *Acts 3:21,* speaks of his stay in heaven until the restitution of all things. Then he will be sent back to earth at a future time. Therefore, this is a prophetic or eschatological statement,bearing upon the future.

NATIONAL REFRESHMENT

Now let us analyze the word *"restitution."* This word is used in the context of Peter's address to Israel , *Acts 3:12,"* Ye men of Israel." The word, *"Restitution"*, in Greek here is, *apokathistemi* (ap-ok-ath-is-tay-mee) meaning **to restore.** In Hebrew,the word is, *Shalam,* (shaw-lam) meaning to **restore, or complete.** This refers to the national refreshment,or restoration of National Israel and the Kingdom of Israel restored. **Times of refreshing.**

📖 **Acts 3:19,** *"Repent ye therefore, and be converted,that your sins may be blotted out, when the*

> *times of refreshing shall come from the presence of the Lord."*

The restitution of all things. What things? **All things.** *"Things"* here in Greek is *pragma,* which means an object, **matter or material.** In Hebrew, or reverted from Greek to Hebrew, the word is, *Keliy,* meaning **vessel, utensil,** a **pot, tool,** etc. All of this related to the great Hebrew Renaissance.

📖 **Hos. 6:2,***"After two days will **He revive us:** in the third day **He will raise us up,** and we shall **live** in His sight."*

📖 **Matt. 19:28,** *"And Jesus said unto them, Verily I say unto you, That ye which have followed me, in the regeneration when the Son of man shall sit on the throne of His glory, ye also shall sit upon twelve thrones, judging the twelve tribes of Israel."*

THE RESTITUTION OF ALL THINGS

What does it require to restore,or establish the Kingdom of Israel as it was in days of old? Can it be done without the Tabernacle as in days of old?

Peter speaks of the restitution of all things.*"Things,"* Acts 3:21,*"* which God hath spoken by the mouth of all His Holy Prophets since the age began" What *"things"* did all the prophets speak of that were to be restored? Who were these prophets speaking to at the time they prophesied? Was it not to the nation of Israel? Were they not prophesying of the scattering and re-gathering of Israel with an eventual full restoration of the Kingdom to Israel? Was the Tabernacle a thing, a material object? Was the ephod a thing?

THE ANOINTING OIL OF MOSES

When the Prophet Moses spoke of the same **Holy Anointing Oil** which he made, being used throughout all of Israel's generations. Was this not a thing, a flask of matter? Is there a generation of Israel still existing today? Yes. Isaiah spoke of the restoration of Zion's walls with the assistance of strangers or Gentiles, *Isa. 60:10,* "And the sons of strangers shall build up thy walls , and their kings shall minister unto thee: for in my wrath I smote thee, but in my favor have I had mercy on thee."

BUILDING THE OLD WASTE PLACES

"*Things*." Building up the old waste places and cities *Isa. 61:4*, "And they shall **build the old wastes,** they shall raise up the former desolation's, and they shall repair the waste cities, the desolation's of many generations." Even the Temple which lay desolate. *Matt.23:37,* "O,Jerusalem, Jerusalem, thou that killest the prophets, and stonest them which are sent unto thee, how often would **I have gathered thy children** together, even as a hen gathereth her chickens under her wings, and ye would not!"

ISRAEL AND THE TABERNACLE RESTORED

Ezekiel prophesied after the national re-establishment of Israel, the tabernacle would be restored. *Ezek. 37:26-28,* "Moreover, I will make a covenant of peace with them; it shall be an everlasting covenant with them: and I will place them, and multiply them, and will set my sanctuary in the midst of them for evermore. **My tabernacle also shall be with them:** yea, I will be their God, and they shall be my people. And the heathen shall know that I the Lord do sanctify Israel, when **my sanctuary shall be in the midst**

63

of them for evermore.'' Even the Priesthood from the Kohen's or **Priests of Zadok would be restored,***Ezek. 44:15.* Hosea, another prophet of Israel speaks of **the restoration of the ephod** *,Hos. 3:4-5* The revival of Israel, *Hos. 6:2-3 , Joel 2:25-28.*

📖 **Amos 9:11,''***In that day will **I raise up the tabernacle of David that is fallen,** and close up the breaches thereof; and I will raise up his ruins, and **I will build it as in the days of old:''**

THE KINGDOM IS COMPLETE WHEN THE KING RETURNS

📖 **Micah 4:8,** *"And thou, 0 tower of the flock, the stronghold of the daughter of Zion, unto thee shall it come, even the first dominion; **the kingdom shall come to the daughter of Jerusalem.''***

ISRAEL AND THE JUBILEE YEARS

Is there a connection between the restitution of all things pertaining to Israel,and the Jubilee years of Israel? Every 50th year in Israel was a Jubilee year. The calendar of Israel was based upon the number seven. Numbers are built into the Hebrew System. The prophet *Daniel* used prophetic numerology, but it was based upon Gods word to Israel. Notice here in the *Book of Daniel* time, times and a half a time. 1,260 days, 42 months, 31/2 years. 1,290 days, and 1,335 days, referring to the future period of the great tribulation, *Rev. 11,12,13, Dan. 7* and *12.* Daniel uses the **Jubilee Cycle** as 70 weeks of years, and the **Sabbatical Cycle** of the 7 year week and the 7 times 7 sabbatical year week, equaling 49 years. *Dan. 9:24-27.*Daniel based this on the **Jubilee Cycle.**

THE JUBILEE CYCLE

📖 **Lev. 25:1-13,** ¹*"And the Lord spake unto Moses in Mount Sinai, saying,*²*Speak unto the children of Israel, and say unto them, When ye come into the land which I give you, then shall the land keep a Sabbath unto the Lord.* ³*Six years thou shalt sow thy field, and six years thou shalt prune thy vineyard, and gather in the fruit thereof;* ⁴*But in the **seventh year shall be a Sabbath of rest unto the land, a Sabbath for the Lord:** thou shalt neither sow thy field, nor prune thy vineyard.* ⁵*That which groweth of its own accord of thy harvest thou shalt not reap, neither gather the grapes of thy vine undressed: it is a year of rest unto the land.* ⁶*And the Sabbath of the land shall be meat for you; for thee, and for thy servant, and for thy maid, and for thy hired servant, and for thy stranger that sojourneth with thee,* ⁷*And for thy cattle, and for the beasts, that are in thy land, shall all the increase thereof be meat.* ⁸***And thou shalt number seven Sabbaths of years unto thee, seven times seven years; and the space of the seven Sabbaths of years shall be unto thee forty and nine years.*** ⁹*Then shalt thou **cause the trumpet of the jubilee to sound** on the tenth day of the seventh month, in the day of atonement shall ye make the trumpet sound throughout all your land.* ¹⁰*And ye shall **hallow the fiftieth year**, and **proclaim liberty** throughout all the land unto all the inhabitants thereof: **it shall be a jubilee unto you**; and ye shall return every man unto his possession, and ye shall return every man unto his family.* ¹⁰ *jubilee shall **that fiftieth year** be unto you: ye shall not sow, neither reap that which groweth of itself in it, nor gather in it the grapes of thy vine undressed.* ¹²*For it is the **jubilee; it shall be holy unto you:** ye shall eat the increase thereof out of the field.*

13In the year of this jubilee ye shall return every man unto his possession. "

Every seventh day was a Sabbath day. Every seventh year was a Sabbath year, after every seventh sabbatical year, in the 50th year was a **Jubilee Year**. In the 50th year **all debts were canceled,** and everyone who had lost their land through debts had their land or **property redeemed** and returned to them or their heirs. **The land rested** for two years, the 49th and 50th years. (Read the full 25th Chapter of Lev.) This applied to the property redemption laws for individuals and families.

THE NATIONAL JUBILEE FOR THE NATIONAL REDEMPTION OF ISRAEL

According to the scriptures, related to *Acts 3:20-21,* which we have explored in this chapter, there is such a National Jubilee for Israel. That all things pertaining to the Kingdom of Israel would be restored as the prophets have spoken. What Jubilee is this and when does it occur? Will it too occur chronologically in this, our generation? The same generation in which Israel became a Nation-State? The same generation in which Historic Jerusalem was restored? If it does, and if this is the 70th Jubilee in Israel's history, then the 70th Jubilee would be this **National or Golden Jubilee** in Israel's history of Jubilees, the national restoration of the Kingdom of Israel.

THE JUBILEE OF 700 BC.

During the reign of King Hezekiah, *2 Kings 19:29,* "And this shall be a sign unto thee, Ye shall eat this year such things as grow of themselves, and in the second year that which springeth of the same; and in the third year sow ye, and reap, and plant vineyards, and eat the fruits thereof."

Only during a Jubilee did the land rest two years. If we count down from this Jubilee, 55 Jubilees, we come to the year 1996. 55 times 49 = 2,695 years. 2,695 years added to 700 B. C. equals 1996. 2,695 - 700 = 1995. THIS BRINGS US TO THE BEGINNING OF 1996. THE JEWISH YEAR BEGINS IN SEPTEMBER. SEPT. 1996 WOULD BE THE BEGINNING.

THE ACCEPTABLE YEAR OF THE LORD

Let us double check,Jesus came to proclaim the **acceptable year of the Lord** or a Jubilee, since his message released the captives, debtors and *brought liberation.* The 30th Jubilee occurred the year of His crucifixion , 34-35 AD.

Jesus is quoting from *Isa. 61 : 1-2.* He closed the book. *Isa. 61 verse 4-5,* deals with the restoration of Israel and their desolation's. Jesus reserves this for later. Therefore, there is a gap of nearly 2,000 years to the National Jubilee of Israel. Forty additional Jubilees,bringing us to the 70th Jubilee of National Israel,that would occur 1,961 years later, about **1996.** Judah was in Babylonian captivity 70 years. Every year represents a Jubilee year to the full restoration of National Israel, *Jer. 25:10-11.*

THE JUBILEE CHART

The countdown of Jubilees begins when Israel conquered and divided the land titles. It began 13 years into the land of Canaan, when Israel had rest, or Sabbath in the land.1435 BC. Thus the 50th year was the first actual Jubilee, or 1386 BC. 1656 years from Adam to the flood -

Gen. 5-6.
> 352 years flood to birth of Abraham.

Gen. 10-11.
> 100 years to birth of Isaac, five years to the weaning of Isaac when his persecution begins of bondage

Gen.21.
> 400 years of oppression and bondage.

> 40years in the wilderness.

13 years in conquering and dividing the land of Canaan.2566 years total 4,000 years Adam to birth of Jesus.

4,000 - 2,566   1,434-35 BC.

THE JUBILEE CHART

1	- 1435 BC - Beginning	36	-	329
2	- 1386	37	-	378
3	- 1337	38	-	427
4	- 1239 Rome Destroyed	39	-	476
5	- 1190	40	-	525
6	- 1141	41	-	574
7	- 1092	42	-	623
8	- 1043	43	-	672
9	- 994	44	-	721
10	- 945	45	-	770
11	- 896	46	- -	819
12	- 847	47	-	868
13	- 798	48	-	917
14	- 749	49	-	996
15	- 700 Hezekiah	50		1015
16	- 651 (2Kings19)	51		1064
17	- 602	52	- -	1113
18	- 553	53	-	1162
19	- 504	54	-	1211
20	- 455	55	-	1260
21	- 406	56	-	1309
22	- 357	57	-	1358
23	- 308	58	-	1407
24	- 259	59	-	1456
25	- 210	60	-	1505
26	- 161	61	-	1554
27	- 112	62	-	1603
28	- 63	63	-	1652
29	- 14	64	-	1701
30	- 35 AD. - Crucifixion	65	-	1750
31	- 84	66	-	1799
32	- 133	67	-	1848
33	- 182	68	-	1897
34	- 231	69	-	1946
35	- 280	70	-	1995

A TRIPLE CHECK

Let us triple check our Jubilee chronology. The National State of Israel was restored May 14, 1948 or the Jewish year 5708. The Jewish year begins in Tishri, or our Sept. 1947 was the beginning of the Jewish year 5708. (check the Jewish calendar) The UN. established the Israel Partition Nov. 1947. Add 49 years to 1947. 1947 + 49 = 1996

SEPTEMBER 1996

BEGINNING OF THE NEXT JUBILEE.

THE ORIGIN AND CONTINUITY OF THE HEBREW LANGUAGE

Chapter Seven

It is commonly thought by many that Jesus and the disciples spoke Aramaic as the language of their day.

ONE LANGUAGE, ONE SPEECH

First of all, I believe the original language was **Hebrew.** It is written in *Gen. 11:1, "And the whole earth was of one language, and of one speech."* The Hebrew language, I believe, was the **seed of all languages.** In the diffusion of languages from the Tower of Babel, the original human intelligence has been preserved in the Hebrew language, giving it's crystal clear structure that dominates the formation of the words. Hebrew is connected with almost every branch of the Semitic Languages and even compared with ancient Babylonian, it has preserved the more original structure. Linguistic evidence has clearly established a relationship between the Hamitic and Semitic peoples. It is also possible to link Semitic and Inda - European languages directly.

Examples: Father - Pater - Pitor - Vater.
Mother - Mater - Mator - Muther - Mere.

Notice the resemblance between Hebrew and Greek letters.

HEBREW	GREEK
ALEPH	ALPHA
BET	BETA
GIMEL	GAMMA
DALET	DELTA
KAPH	KAPPA
LAMED	LAMBDA
MEM	UM
NUN	NU

71

Refer to the <u>Universal Jewish History</u> by Rabbi Philip Biberfeld L.L.D. 1948 , the Spero Foundation. Also,the book of <u>Jewish Knowledge</u> by Nathan Ausubel , Crown Publishers, Inc. New York.

There were 160 cities with Hebrew names in the land of Canaan before the birth of Abraham, as recorded in Egyptian language records. They are listed in <u>The Lands of the Bible,</u> by Yohanon Aharoni.

The Hebrew language existed long before the sons of Abraham. The Hittites, Philistines, Moabites and Canaanites, spoke a similar language or different, dialects of it. This was confirmed by the Moabite Stone, which was inscribed with the victories of Moabite King Mesho, over King Ahab of Israel. The inscription was in a language reminiscent of Biblical Hebrew. The Hebrew language is called **Ivrit,** or the **social language**, *Lashon ha - kodesh.* It is called the language of Canaan, by *Isaiah 19:18.*

We must ask ourselves what language God spoke from the heavenlies, and what was the language from the Garden of Eden to the Tower of Babel? There is a direct line of communications from the Garden of Eden to Abraham.

Adam lived 243 years after Methuselah was born. Methuselah lived 600 years after Noah was born, and 98 years after Abraham entered Canaan. Abraham was called "the Hebrew" and was the offspring of Eber, of the lineage of Shem, *Gen. 11:11-26,Gen. 14:13.* The Hebrew language, or Ivrit was passed on to Isaac, Jacob and the 12 sons of Jacob. Jesus did not speak Aramaic, Greek or English. **The Jewish identity of Jesus still echos in the Hebrew language to our generation.**

THE PROPHETS THAT SPOKE HEBREW

A commonly accepted view is that the Hebrew language was lost during the Babylonian captivity, and that a Gentile language, Aramaic replaced it. Biblical, historical and archeological evidence counteracts this attempt to supersede the Hebrew language and culture. The truth is, the **post-Babylonian captivity Prophets, Haggai, Zechariah, Ezra, Nehemiah, Malachi and even Daniel wrote in Hebrew.** There are Aramaic words in these books, but they are written for the most part in Hebrew, proving it was not lost. You will see and hear Latin and even French words in English today, but that does not prove the English language is lost. The Aramaic languages originated from the offspring of Aram, *Gen.10:22*, while **Hebrew came from Eber,** *Gen. 10:24.* A Bible writer, occasionally using an Arabic or Aramaic word doesn't prove that he does not speak Hebrew, anymore than if I used a French or Latin word proves I don't speak English.

The book of *Daniel, chapters 2:4 to 7:28* is in Aramaic. The other parts are in Hebrew. Much of the Second through Seventh Chapters of Daniel concerned the Gentile language, Chaldaic - Aramaic, but *Chapters 8-12* were related to Israel and the End-time, so he wrote in Hebrew. *Ezra 4:18-6:18 and 7:12-26,*Ezra writes, in Aramaic because this text is composed of a message from Israel's enemies. The balance of Ezra is written in Hebrew which was still alive and active. Ezra explained why he used Aramaic in these special portions of the text, in *Ezra 4:7.*

Nehemiah rebuked those Jews who married strange wives, and polluted the Hebrew language with Ashdodic, Moabic and other Arabic languages,while there is no mention of pollution by Aramaic, *Neh.13:23-24.* The Hebrew language was preserved through 400 years of Egyptian influence, and it was preserved through the shorter span of 70 years Babylonian captivity.

The Maccabean revolution prevented the Hebrew language from being swallowed up by the Greek language. The Maccabeans were intent on sifting all Greek and other foreign words from the Hebrew language. Josephus wrote his Jewish history in Greek because he was writing for the benefit of the Greco-Roman world. The <u>Dead Sea Scrolls</u> were discovered beginning about 1947. They contain many Old Testament scriptures and Qumran teachings that were written during the period 150-200 years before the birth of Jesus. They are all written in Hebrew, not Aramaic. This proves the **Hebrew language was active in the Second Temple period, up to the birth of Jesus.**

THE LANGUAGE OF JESUS' DAY WAS HEBREW

There are numerous documents proving **the language of Jesus' day was Hebrew.** Documents translated by I.T. Milik, M. Baillet, and R.De Vauxop Oxford 1962, are a few examples: The script of the <u>Uzziah Plaque</u> AD 50;The script of the <u>Copper Document</u> found in Cave III. A late <u>Herodian Script</u> AD 50-68, from an unpublished manuscript of <u>Psalms</u> from Cave IV, Qumran.

A post-Herodian Biblical land, AD 70-100. From fragments of a <u>Biblical Scroll,</u> preserved by members of a camp of Bar Kochba, from an unidentified site. A semi-formal script, from a Hebrew contract, dated AD 133. **Pilate wrote a title** and put it on the cross. The writing was, **"Jesus of Nazareth, the King of the Jews." It was written in Hebrew, Greek, and Latin.** Notice, it was not written in Aramaic. Does this indicate that Hebrew, or Aramaic ,was the common language in Israel in the days of Jesus and the disciples? *St. John 19:17,19-20,* Jesus was crucified at the place called *"Skull"*, which is called *Golgotha,* in Hebrew.

The "*Messiah*," which is being interpreted, **The Christ**. *Ha Mah Shi YKH*, the **anointed.** The word Messiah,originated in Hebrew, *St. John 1:41.* A *"pool,"* which is called in the Hebrew tongue, *Bethesda, St. John 5:2. St. John 19:13,* called the *"Pavement,"* but in the Hebrew also *Gabbatha. Heb. 7:2,*Melchizedek, King of Salem, King of Peace in Hebrew. *Rev. 9:11,* whose name in the Hebrew tongue is Abaddon. Rev.16:16, a place called in the Hebrew tongue, Armageddon. Jerome in the 3rd Century AD. studied Hebrew for 14 years in Tiberias so he could translate the Old and New Testaments from Hebrew into Latin.

In *Acts 21:37 to 22:2,* **Paul is speaking** to the people, not in Greek or in Aramaic,but **in Hebrew.** The Roman Emperor Hadrain issued his edict against the Hebrew language, how could he have done this, if the Hebrew language did not exist at that time? Dr. David Flusser,of Hebrew University says, "Jesus and his disciples spoke Hebrew if he lived in Eretz Yisrael 2,000 years ago."

TWENTIETH CENTURY HEBREW

In the period which followed the Old Testament Prophets, a century or two before the destruction of the Second Temple, by the Romans in 70 AD, Meshnic Hebrew emerged. This was the language in which the Mishnah, the code of oral law, was written. This was the common language of the people. There were Aramaic words added to this Hebrew. After the destruction of Jerusalem, Mishnic Hebrew began to die a lingering death. This was caused by the global dispersion of the Jews, the rising dominance of Aramaic and those hostile to the Jewish people,who wanted to destroy all vestiges of Hebrew Culture. Yet, in the Jewish prayers and Torah, **Hebrew continued to be used. It simply refused to remain dead.** The Hebrew language, in the 20th, century arose from the dead, with Israel.

Eliezer Ben Yehudah (1858-1922), **was the Father of Hebrew,** in our modern world. He worked toward establishing Hebrew as a modern language. From *Ezek. 37:7,* which is translated in the Hebrew Text:

> *VaYHieY* - and it was
> *QoHL* - a voice
> *KHinahVieY* - as my voice echo
> *W'HiNaeH* - and see
> *Rash* - a stirring
> *WaTiqRvou* - and they re gathered
> *aTSAHMoHI* - Together again
> *GehTsehM* - Her Bones as bones
> *QehL* - onto
> *GATSMOH* - His bones

This refers to the *"re-establishment"* of Israel, the *"recovery"* of the Temple Vessels, and *"restoration"* of the Tabernacle, all from the Hebrew Word, *Tiqrvou.*

SIGNS OF THE SEASON
MATTHEW 24

Chapter Eight

Actually, this discourse by Jesus began in the 23rd chapter of Matthew. It is important for us to determine the theme of the message here in order to comprehend all the parts.

DESTRUCTION OF THE TEMPLE

In *Matt. 23*, Jesus is rebuking the Pharisees, not Israel and only the Phariseeical religion, in general for their failures and consequent corruption. In *verse 34* of *Matt. 23,* he turns his attention to their coming judgment. As a part of that judgment, those who had defiled the temple and themselves, were bringing about the destruction of the temple.

📖 **Matt. 23:38-39,** *"Behold your house is left unto you desolate. For I say unto you, ye shall not see me henceforth, till ye shall say, Blessed is he that cometh in the name of the Lord."*

Then in *Matt. 24:1,* Jesus departed from the temple. The temple had been the topic of the dialogue, illustrating its destruction. Then his disciples came to him to show him the buildings of the temple. Temple *"buildings"*, plural.

📖 **Matt. 24:2,** *"and Jesus said unto them, See ye not all these things? Verily I say unto you, There shall not be left here one stone upon another, that shall not be thrown down."*

Jesus now is still speaking of the destruction of the temple buildings. They are standing there looking at them. *Matt. 24:3* "and as he sat upon the Mount of Olives, the disciples

came unto him privately, saying, Tell us, when shall these things be?
What shall be the sign of thy coming and of the end of the world?" It is important to understand, the **disciples were asking Jesus,** two major questions. **When** will these things be, referring to the destruction of the temple.**What** shall be the sign of thy coming and of the end of the world? *"World"*, here is translated in Greek as *aion* or *age*. Unless we believe Jesus came, or returned, two thousand years ago, these two questions cover a period of two thousand years. One question is referring to the events related to the **Destruction of the Temple,** and the other is related to the **Coming of Jesus.** My friends, there is a 2,000 year gap in between.①

THE ABOMINATION OF DESOLATION

Included in the answers Jesus gave the disciples is the preaching of the gospel to all nations and the abomination of desolation spoken of by Daniel the prophet. Daniel's time table is future, beyond even the time of the Apostle John in *Rev. 13,* a **great tribulation** will occur such as not since the beginning of the world.

THE RETURN OF JESUS ,
GOD'S KINGDOM ON EARTH

The **Returning of Jesus Christ,** the budding, not the withering fig tree, the **Times of Gentile Fulfillment,** and then the **visible Demonstration of God's Kingdom on earth** superseding the dominion of worldly kingdoms.

📖 **Luke 21:24, 31** *24"And they shall fall by the edge of the sword, and shall be led away captive into all nations: and Jerusalem shall be trodden down of the Gentiles until the times of the Gentiles be fulfilled.* *31*

So likewise ye, when ye see these things come to pass, know ye that the Kingdom of God is nigh at hand. "

📖 **Dan.** **7:27,** *"And the kingdom and dominion, and the greatness of the **kingdom** under the whole heaven, shall be given to the people of the Saints of the Most High, whose Kingdom is an everlasting Kingdom, and all dominions shall serve and obey Him. "*

📖 **Rev.** **11:15,** *"And the seventh angel sounded; and there were great voices in heaven, saying, The kingdoms of this world are become the Kingdoms of our Lord, and of His Christ; and He shall reign for ever and ever. "*

📖 **Rev. 5:9-10,** *[9]"And they sung a new song, saying, Thou art worthy to take the book, and to open the seals thereof: for thou wast slain, and hast redeemed us to God by thy blood out of every kindred, and tongue, and people, and nation; [10]and hast made us unto our God a Kingdom of Priests: and we shall reign on the earth. "*

This is all included in the answers Jesus gave. It did not all occur in 70 AD. Prior to His Return, we are to teach people to observe all things whatsoever he commanded us.

📖 **Matt. 28:20,***"and lo, he said, I am with you always, even to the end of the world. "*

ISRAEL'S BIRTH PAINS

There were to be birth pains accompanying the birth of Israel, in modern times. Jesus portrays these as signs of the times surrounding the new born nation of Israel. These were to continue until His Return. *Hos. 5:15, Zech. 13:8-9, Zech.14:1-4 .*

The gospel of the Kingdom is expounded to the Nations.There is a universal outpouring of the Holy Spirit, a great harvest, a period of tribulation and then Jesus returns to earth *Matt.24:14-16.*

📖 **Matt.24:29-30,** *"Immediately after the tribulation of those days shall the sun be darkened, and the moon shall not give her light, and the stars shall fall from heaven, and the powers of the heavens shall be shaken:And then shall appear the sign of the Son of man in heaven: and then shall all the tribes of the earth mourn, and they shall see the Son of man coming in the clouds of heaven with power and great glory."*

The Coming of Jesus in Glory occurs immediately after the tribulation. There are many signs portrayed by the prophets and by Jesus relating to our generation and the return of Jesus. Like golden beams of light shining in radiant splendor, and sparkling in all directions, **we witness the signs of His Coming Today.**

📖 **Jer. 31:23,** *"Thus saith the Lord of Hosts, the God of Israel; as yet they shall use this speech in the land of Judah and in the cities there of, when I shall bring again their captivity."*

This scripture is in the context of Israel's return from the nations, or from the global dispersion.

📖 **Jer. 31:8, 34,** *[8]"Behold, I will bring them from the north country, and gather them from the coasts of the earth, and with them the blind and the lame, the woman with child and her that travaileth with child together: a great company shall return thither. [34]And they shall teach no more every man his neighbor, and every man his brother, saying, Know the Lord: for they* *shall all know me, from the least of them unto the greatest of them, saith the Lord: for I will forgive their iniquity, and I will remember their sin no more."*

THE HEBREW LANGUAGE REVIVED

Therefore, when Israel was to be re-gathered from the nations, the speech of Jeremiah, *the Hebrew language was to be restored to the people.* Has this happened? In the 20th century, Ben Yehuda revived the Hebrew language. *In 1981, Hebrew became the official secular language of Israel.* It is spoken in that land today. Hebrew is the only ancient language ever to be restored and spoken.

THE SECOND GREAT EXODUS

📖 **Isa. 43:6,** "I *will say to the north, give up, and to the south, keep not back, bring my sons from far, and my daughters from the ends of the earth."*

The last power to hold Israel is the Soviet Union, the empire to the extreme north. Before 1988, only a few Jews now and then were allowed to leave the Soviet Union. In the year 1988, according to Time Magazine, 8,000 Russian Jews were allowed to emigrate. During the first six months of 1989, twenty thousand were allowed to leave the Soviet Union. By 1990, according to the Associated Press and Religious News Service, ten thousand per month were leaving. A total of 178,000 Jews were released from the north in 1990. In Oct. 1990, Mikhail Gorbachev, Chief of State of the Soviet Union, announced Jewish emigration would be accelerated even more. **Since 1990, over 450,000 Soviet Jews have been released, tens of thousands returning to Israel.** Approximately another million are still in the Former Soviet Republics. *We are witnessing the greatest exodus since the time of Moses.* The timing of the

81

the temple treasures and the tabernacle emergence. Israel looks forward to the,*Oligot,* the time of the *Great Celebration.* **This great exodus is a sort of repeat of history, as Israel's exodus from Egypt.** Later, Russia will pursue them and be swallowed up in the valley of Hamongog, by the Dead Sea, *Ezek. 39:11.*

THE DESERT BLOSSOMS

Today, the Judean Desert is beginning to blossom like a rose. For the first time in history, a vineyard grows in the Valley of Achor, of the Judean Desert.*The former and latter rains have returned to the desert,* as I have personally witnessed while living in the desert. In some places in Israel today, they grow five to seven crops each year on the same piece of ground. The rains have returned all the way to the Negev.

📖 **Amos 9:13,** *"Behold, the days come, saith the Lord, that the plowman shall overtake the reaper, and the treader of grapes him that soweth seed; and the mountains shall drop sweet wine, and all the hills shall melt."*

Israel produces enough fruit for the entire Middle - East, and exports more to Western Europe then all Western Europe produces. Israel now exports about 80% of its fruit and vegetables. To think only a few years ago north Israel was a swamp and Judea was a desert. Phenomenal? No! Miraculous? YES!

📖 **Ezek. 36:11,30,34-36,** *[11]I will multiply upon you man and beast; and they shall increase and bring fruit; I will settle you after your old estates, and will do better unto you than at your beginnings: and ye shall know that I am the Lord. [30]And I will multiply the* *fruit of the tree, and the increase of the field, and that ye shall receive **no more reproach of famine** among the heathen. ³⁴And the desolate land shall be tilled, whereas it lay desolate in the sight of all that passed by. ³⁵And they say, this land that was desolate is become **like the Garden of Eden**, and the waste and desolate and ruined cities are become fenced, and are inhabited. ³⁶Then the heathen that are left round about you shall know that I the Lord build, the ruined places, and **plant that which was desolate**. I the Lord, have spoken it, and **I will do it.** "*

Israel will eventually fill the face of the world with fruit. *Isa. 27:6*

THE BIG SEARCH

The big search is under way for the Tabernacle of David and its Priceless Treasures as a sign of our times. There is our project at Qumran and several other projects in the Jerusalem area. *Amos. 9:11-13*

THE MILLENNIAL REIGN

In comparing the events and conditions of the millennial reign of Christ Jesus, such as *Isa. 11:4* with *Rev. 19:15*, the **peaceful environment,** and the **Lord's universal knowledge** Isaiah is describing the millennial reign of Christ. In *Isa. 11:6-10,* He says in the context of that time just prior to that millennial reign, Israel shall be gathered back the second time. *The first time*, all 12 tribes of Israel were scattered after becoming a nation was during the Babylonian captivity. *The second time* was the dispersion following 70 AD. *Isa. 11:11-12,* " And it shall come to pass in that day, that the Lord shall set his hand again the second time to recover the remnant of his people which he left,

83

from Assyria (Iraq) and from Egypt, and from Pathros (Southern Egypt) and from Cush, (Ethiopia) and from Elam (Iran) and from Shinar (Southern Iraq and Kuwait) and from Hamath (Syria) and from the isles of the sea. Isles of the Gentiles or of Tarshish, including the United States and the British Isles, *Ezek. 38:13, Ps.72:10-11, Gen. 10:5.*② On May 25, 1991 Israel airlifted 18,006 Ethiopian Jews from Cush, or Ethiopia, back into Israel.

FLY UPON THE SHOULDERS OF THE PHILISTINES

📖 **Isa. 11:14,***"They shall fly upon the shoulders of the Philistines,"*

Today, Israel's main airport, the International Airport at Tel Aviv, is located right on the upper part, or **shoulder part,** of the ancient territory *of the Philistines.* So Israel is literally *flying upon the shoulders* of the Philistines.

A great universal outpouring of the Holy Spirit was to occur following Israel's restoration, *Joel 2:25-28.*The major part of this outpouring is yet to come. A great spiritual outpouring and harvest was to come just prior to the return of Jesus. *James 5:7-8, Matt. 18:47, 49.*

THE CRY OF PEACE AND SAFETY

This cry is prevalent throughout the land, *1 Thess. 5:1-2.* This is a sign pointing to the Lord's Coming as a thief in the night, *1 Thess. 5:1-4.* There is a certain apathy, indifference, or slumbering on the part of many Christian people today. Will we have revival or apostasy? The answer is, yes. We will have both. A revival , a harvest, and a falling away. Light and darkness which has existed since the beginning of time. We have both revival and apostasy now.

84

APOSTASY, MODERNISM, HUMANISM

While thousands are turning to Christ Jesus, especially in Africa, Asia and in such South American countries as Brazil, we also have apostasy, modernism, humanism. Humanism, embracing the devil's first lie, *"ye shall be as Gods,"* Gen. 3:5, is raising its ugly head, deceiving, infiltrating most every segment of society.

TECHNOLOGY IS MULTIPLYING

📖 **Dan. 12:4,** *"But thou, O Daniel, shut up the words, and seal the book, even to the time of the end: many shall run to and fro, and **knowledge shall be increased.** "*

In only 1-1/2 % of the total span of 6,000 years from Adam, practically all modern inventions have been developed. This includes the automobile, airplane, penicillin, jet engines, rockets, radio, television, motion pictures, and computers. In many aspects, we are moving toward a one-world government.

We are a smaller, more inter-dependent world. Each nation is more interrelated by trade, communications, and technology and through world organizations such as the UN and its varied branch agencies, common-markets and regional blocs.

📖 **Rev. 13:2,** *"And the beast which I saw was like unto a leopard, and his feet were as the feet of a bear, and his mouth as the mouth of a lion: and the dragon gave him his power, and his seat, and great authority."*

📖 **Dan. 2:43,** *"And whereas thou sawest iron mixed with miry clay, they shall mingle themselves with the seed of*

85

men: but they shall not cleave one to another, even as iron is not mixed with clay."

WARS AND RUMORS OF WARS

Why should I disbelieve we are moving into a one world society when **our own US. President witnesses wars and has referred to the new world order now in existence on the national news.** Rumors of wars around the globe, particularly in the Middle-East, more frequently. It is reported 1-1/2 billion people in the world are malnourished. With nearly a billion hungry, famine is wider spread and more **intense with changing weather** and climate patterns. **Earthquakes in diverse places,** are **now occurring** during major changes, and shifts among the nations, **while wars and rumors of war rage in the Middle East, surrounding Israel.** Sometimes, two or three earthquakes occur near together in separate parts of the world and with greater frequency, just like *birth or labor pains.*

There are cults, false christs, and satan worship, all paving the way for anti-Christ, or Mashiach Megid ; the negative Messiah. *Dan. 9:27, Matt. 24:24, 2 Thess. 2:3-12, Rev. 9:20.* Hurricanes or whirlwinds are being raised up more frequently and with greater force upon the coasts of the earth,*Jer. 25:32*

The kings of the East are already emerging, *Rev.16:14,* Japan is now dominant in world finance. Drugs and social permissiveness are epidemic. Aids and mystifying diseases are rampant, *Luke 21:8-11.* Yet I am not a pessimist, seeing all this turmoil today as the death rattles of an old age. I am an optimist in Christ Jesus, I see it as the birth pains of a **New Golden Era.**

📖 *Luke 21:28,* "And when these things begin to come to pass, then **look up**, and **lift up your heads**; for your **redemption draweth nigh.**"

END-TIME ALIGNMENT OF
NATIONS

Chapter Nine

As of 1990, *Daniel 2:31-44*, is now beginning to come into plain focus. In the second chapter of Daniel, Nebuchadnezzar, the King of Babylon, more than five hundred years before the birth of Christ Jesus, had a dream. Nebuchadnezzar could not remember or interpret the dream. Eventually, Daniel, the Hebrew Prophet, was called upon to interpret the dream. Nebuchadnezzar had dreamed of an image in the shape of a man, or the anatomy of the human body. The various parts of the image were composed of different metals. The head was of gold, the shoulders, arms and chest of silver, belly of brass, legs of iron, feet part of iron and part of clay and toes part of iron and part clay. The image, as was explained to Nebuchadnezzar by Daniel, represented the history of the Gentile world, or the unfolding of the major Gentile Kingdoms.

The dream begins with Babylon because it was the first Gentile Kingdom that destroyed, and trod the city of Jerusalem under foot. Therefore, in Daniel's time, Babylon was relevant to the destruction and captivity of Jerusalem. For us this sets a measuring system for **"the Times of the Gentiles"**, as we shall see, *Luke 21:24*.

📖 **2 Chron. 36:19-21,** [19]*"And they burned the house of God and broke down the wall of Jerusalem, and burned all the palaces thereof with fire, and destroyed all the goodly vessels. [20]And those who had escaped from the sword carried he away to Babylon, where they were servants to him and his sons until the reign of the kingdom of Persia, [21]To fulfill the word of the Lord by the mouth of Jeremiah, until the land had enjoyed her Sabbaths; for as long as she lay desolate she kept the Sabbath, to fulfill threescore and ten years."*

DANIEL'S INTERPRETATION

Babylon was **the head of gold,** *Dan. 2:38.* Persia was the silver.

The Greco-Macedonian Empire under Alexander the Great was **the brass.***Dan.8:20-21*

The kingdom that followed Greece was the Roman Empire, the **legs of iron.** Since there are two legs that divide, the Roman Empire eventually divided into the Eastern and Western Empires, 395 AD. The Roman Empire was ruling when Jesus was born in Bethlehem, *Luke 2:1.* **The feet and toes** were yet to come, for the end was not yet.

Just as there are joints between these major parts of the human body, there were transitions between each great Gentile Kingdom. During those transitions were upheaval, revolutions, and wars. These transitions are represented by **the neck, the rib cage, the hip joint, the knee, the ankles, and finally the joints between the feet and toes.**

THE END-TIME

When you reach the feet, you are at the end of the body and at the end of the toes. Well, that is the end of the body. Where are we now? In the words of Jesus, *Luke 21:24,* Jerusalem shall be trodden down of the Gentiles until the times of the Gentiles be fulfilled. Actually, the first Gentile Kingdom that trod Jerusalem under foot was Babylon, the head of gold. **At the pivot point in Gentile history, when old Jerusalem is liberated from Gentile dominion, would be the fulfilling of the Times of the Gentiles, or the final generation of Gentiles or worldly rule.** This pivot point was **June of 1967.** Since that time Jerusalem has been the

89

Solo Rex Capital of a United Israel. Therefore during the Six Days War of 1967, the world passed through the ankle joints into the feet. **The absolute end-time**.

THE ONE WORLD ORDER

Since that time we have been moving toward a one world economy.This "one world financial system"is characterized by international banks and multi-national corporations which recognize no national boundaries to their business.

The system is also composed of Regional and International Trade Blocs and Conferences, UN, Political and Military control, and such organizations as the Trilateral Commission.

Then in 1987, we begin to witness the unprecedented, rapid **revolutionary changes in the climate of world affairs.** We witnessed the signing of the I.N.F. Treaty. The I.N.F. Treaty (Intermediate Ballistic Missiles) was to remove missiles and nuclear forces from Eastern and Western Europe, thus reducing the danger of invasion by either East or West. The subsequent disarmament agreements, combined with Eastern Europe becoming more independent of the Soviet Union, makes it possible for Europe to become more neutral and for the drawing together of a **cohesive East - West Europe**.

Thus, in accordance with the designs of the Vatican and various leaders of Europe, **A Pan-European Alliance** is being formed. All of this also paved the way for the **re-unification of Germany**. Germany will ultimately take a more neutralist position. We witnessed a sudden display of openness and **change in Russia** and the change from a party controlled government to a Presidential controlled government. This was quickly followed by the domino like

90

succession of **falling communist parties in Eastern European countries.**

Poland, East Germany, Czechoslovakia, Romania, Hungary and others. Soviet Republics also declared their independence from Russia, with others demanding more freedom.

Our own **US. President George Bush,** has declared, that **a new world order** has emerged. He declared, "**the world is witnessing** the cooperation of this **new world order,** through the multi-National forces in Saudi Arabia."

Western Europe is scheduled to become a cohesive bloc by Dec. 1992, by removing the boundary lines of the nations in that region, forming a United States of Europe,as the legs of iron were the West - East Roman Empire and Rome gave way to the Nationalistic States.

The feet and toes are an extension of the legs, and the nationalist states are forming new alliances, or Political , Social - Economic Blocs,since a new world order, is being formed. With all the other evidence we have mentioned, we surely are seeing today the formation of a **new world order** composed of the **East - West Power Blocs,** or the ten toes of the two feet. The two feet just as the human feet, will cooperate temporarily to carry the body. In this case, **the head or mind of Babylon,** and the **spirit of Rome.** Notice the whole Gentile body stood until the very end and the "*Stone Kingdom*" judged and smashed the system, and supersedes it. **Jesus Christ is that Corner Stone.**

Thus, the head of Gold, the mind of Babylon, influences the world with humanism, cults, new age thinking of Persia violence, Greece of arrogance, astrology, humanism, sex art, etc. Rome of iron rule, harshness, Napoleanic law and clay or deteriorated, fragmented societies, etc. The clay is systems that are flexible. Clay is flexible. You can mold and shape it any way you want. You have a blend here of a Roman, dictatorial, socialistic, democratic system blended still further with the seeds of men, or **humanism.** The devil's first lie, *"If you eat of this tree, you (humans) will be as Gods." Gen. 3:5, "For God doth know that in the day ye eat thereof, then your eyes shall be opened, and ye **shall be as gods,** knowing good and evil." Dan. 2:43, "And whereas thou sawest iron mixed with miry clay, they shall **mingle themselves with the seed of men**: but they shall not cleave one to another, even as iron is not mixed with clay."*

THREE MAJOR COMPONENTS

Thus, the world is moving into a one world system consisting of three major component parts. A one world **political** structure, a one world **religious** system, and a one world **financial** system, all to be eventually ruled over by the anti-Christ.

Mr. Bush has acknowledged the **New World Political System,** as have other heads of state. The world economy is controlled by the heads of the multi-national corporations, who are not restricted by national boundaries, and all these are **infiltrated and blended with** those adhering to the so-called **new age philosophies,** and there are also the **very liberal world church organizations,** and the religious leaders in Europe that have influenced the formation of a **Pan-European Alliance.** The varied ethnic groups, and other interests will not hold together with the **iron and clay.**
Rev. 13, portrays a world order ruled over by the antiChrist. *Rev. 18,* describes a world system of International Trade, consisting of all nations, which eventually collapses in one hour. *Babylon is fallen, is fallen.* Babylon fell twice.

Once, natural Babylon, and the second time, the world order influenced by the mind of ancient Babylon, which was the **mother of humanism, astrology and even witchcraft and the so-called New Age Movement.**

GLOBAL ECONOMY

In *Proverbs 1,* it is projected, they shall say, *"Let us all have one purse,"* a ten toed World Kingdom consisting of East-West. The Berlin Wall separated East and West. The **crumbling of the Wall signified the Union of East and West, with iron and clay.** Socialism, or State control, from the Roman spirit and the clay of pluralism, or Democracy, blended together. The trend today is very clearly moving in the direction for the **emergence of a One World Order, from the end of the cold war.** We now move toward the **International cry of Peace and Safety,** *1 Thess. 5:1-5.* We are clearly witnessing the **globalization of the Economy.**

📖 **Rev. 13:2,7,8,17,** *2"And **the beast** which I saw was like a leopard, and his feet were as the feet of a bear, and his mouth as the mouth of a lion: 7and the dragon gave him his power, and his seat, and great authority.And it was given unto him to make war with the saints, and to overcome them; and power was given him over **all kindreds, and tongues, and nations.** 8and all that dwell upon the earth shall worship him, whose names are not written in the book of life of the Lamb slain from the foundation of the world. 17And that no man might buy or sell, save he that had the mark, or the name of the beast, or the number of his name."* *Rev, 18:2,3,9, Dan. 11:36-38, Rev. 13:18, Rom. 1:25.* Read Prophecy 2000 by Dr. David Lewis, on the New Age Movement.

In 1989/90, European leaders themselves were saying that Europe will be the center of a world order which will usher in a Golden Age by the year 2,000. Thus,the feet of the Image is a spread of the Roman Empire to world-wide dimensions. **Five blocs in the East and five major blocs in the West. Rev. Chapter 18 portrays a one world trade system composed of all nations, called mystical Babylon. The Gatt talks in Uruguay are negotiating a one world trade pact. The G-7 group is the frame work for such a system.**

The Gatt conferences (General Agreement for Trade and Tariffs) are negotiating a one world trade system. The Club of Rome composed of top leaders in the European Union have proposed dividing the whole world into ten major regions. Ten horns of the dragon, and the dragon's tail will stretch all the way to China.

JESUS THE STONE
THE BUILDER'S REJECTED

The **stone was cut** out of the mountain **without hands**, or the human, *Dan. 2:43.* That stone is the **stone of stumbling,** the **rock of offense,** the stone the builders rejected.

📖 **1Pet. 2:4-8,** *"To whom coming, as **unto a living stone**, disallowed indeed of men, but **chosen of God**, and precious, Ye also, as **lively stones**, are built up a **spiritual house, a holy priesthood,** to offer up spiritual sacrifices, acceptable to **God by Jesus Christ.** Wherefore also it is contained in the scripture, Behold, **I lay in Zion a chief corner stone,** elect, precious: and he that believeth on him shall not be confounded. Unto you therefore which believe he is precious: but unto them which be disobedient, the stone which the builders disallowed the same is made the head of the corner, and a rock of offense, even to them which stumble at the word, being disobedient: whereunto also they were appointed."*

94

The "stone" the builders of today's New Gentile World Order, are still rejecting.That is **Jesus Christ, the Prince of Peace.**

📖 **Rom. 8:16-17,** ¹⁶"*The spirit itself beareth witness with our spirit, that we are the children of God: And if children, then heirs¹⁷heirs of God, and joint-heirs with Christ; if so be that we suffer with him, that we may be also glorified together.*"

That is the "**stone**" of the Messianic Kingdom, including the "**saints**" who are joint heirs with Jesus Christ, to render judgment upon the feet of the image , *Jude 14* , and the ten toes ,or kingdoms of this world. **The "stone" became a great mountain that filled the Earth,** this is that **Messianic Kingdom.**

📖 **Rev. 11:15**, "*And the seventh angel sounded; and there were great voices in heaven, saying, the kingdoms of this world are become the kingdoms of our Lord, and of his Christ; and he shall reign for ever and ever.*"

RUSSIA

Russia has acted largely because of facing economic ruin, unable to permanently sustain her powerful military machine, and support Eastern Europe. She needs finance, trade and technology from the western world.

A weaker Russia is not necessarily a safer Russia. Her **symbol is the bear. Remember this, a wounded bear is extremely dangerous.**

Why the changes in the Soviet Republics and how does this fit into the Prophetic End-time. The **dismantling** of the **Soviet Republics** and the **fall of Communism** in Russia and the Republics **contributes to the formation of a One World Order,** thereby fulfilling Bible Prophecy.

Now Russia and these Republics as a Commonwealth of Independent States are being brought into this **single world market economy,** yet Russia will emerge with a nationalistic fervor. **Russia historically, even under the Czars before Communism, manifested a strong spirit of nationalism and imperialism. A stronger more dictatorial leadership will be exerted in Russia.**

All of the Republics of the Soviet Union do not necessarily invade Israel. According to *Ezek. 38:1-5,* **Rosh or Russia was to lead a Moslem Confederacy against Israel.** Russia, eventually stimulated and agitated by ties with the Fundamentalist Moslem States of the Middle-East, and rising anti-Semitism in Europe, **will invade Israel.** They will also be motivated by, **financial gain, to strengthen their own currency.** *They will invade Israel also for the wealth, Dead sea minerals, or spoils, and the Gold and Silver after the Tabernacle has been restored, Ezek. 37:27-28, 37:13.*

Even now in 1992, Iran is fervently expanding Islam in the former Soviet Republics. **Communism is being replaced by humanism**, influencing a **One World System,** infused with a mixture of **Socialism and Democracy.**

TWO POSITIVE FACTORS

However, the changes occurring in Europe and the Soviet Union in the 1990's is bringing about two factors of a positive nature. **The opening of doors for the preaching of the Gospel** in the former Soviet Republics and Eastern Europe. Just in time for the great harvest of the 1990's, *Matt, 24:14.*

The second positive factor, is **the exodus of the Jewish** people from the Soviet land of the north,fulfilling *Isa. 43:6* "The Lord spoke to the North and said give up oh North, and let this people go". This is already the **greatest Exodus** of Israel since Moses. In 1990, 178,000 left the Soviet Union. By 1992, over 450,000, and a million more on the way. **Tens of thousands settle in Israel.**

Now, the Soviet lands have the largest Moslem population outside the Middle-East.

The Young Lions of Tarshish , *Ezek. 38:11,* represent the trading colonies of the Ancient Phoenicians, who established the great European shipping center known as Tarshish, in Spain. These colonies were what is now known as the United States, Canada and Great Britain.

In Wiseman's, Peoples of Old Testament Times pages 264-65, there is reference to Phoenician Maritime enterprises on the Palermo Stone, inscription 2,200 BC., of forty timber carrying ships from Byblos. It suggests that, by this time,commercial sea going traffic had long been established. In fact, Alabaster vases, bearing Egyptian royal cartouches of the Second Dynasty, have been found in Byblos. Nor were these Fourth Dynasty ships mere boats; the Palermo Stone reveals that the wood carried was for the construction of three ships, each 170 feet long.

There is a multitude of discoveries which prove that the many hitherto mysterious inscriptions discovered in the Americas, are actually traceable to a thousand years of

97

Commerce by Sea between Tarshish in Spain and various Phoenician colonies in what is now the United States.①

At the time Magog invades Israel, there will be peace in Israel because of Israel's agreement with the anti-Christ and world order, *Dan. 9:27, Ezek, 38:11*, the "*Chief Prince*", will come down from the North. Chief Prince in Hebrew is *Rosh,* the feminine form of Russia.

A PATTERN BEING SET
FIRST THE BATTLE, LATER ARMAGEDDON

Sheba and Dedan form a part of Saudi Arabia which is even now a moderate nation toward Israel and more pro-America. **US. forces in 1990 in Saudi Arabia is an example of the pattern being set.** ②"The Battle" described in *Ezek. 38-39,* which Israel will astonishingly win with God's help, involves only the nations mentioned. Therefore, **Armageddon will be a later war** involving the Kings of the East, Europe, the Arab States, Northern Africa, and the anti-Christ and his forces.

📖 **Dan. 11:31-45,** *31 "And arms shall stand on his part, and* ***they shall pollute*** *the* **sanctuary** *of strength, and shall take away the daily sacrifice, and they shall place the* **abomination that maketh desolate.** *32And such as do wickedly against the covenant shall he* **corrupt by flatteries:** *but the people that do know their God shall be strong, and do exploits. 33And they that understand among the people shall instruct many: yet they shall* **fall by the sword**, *and by flame, by* **captivity**, *and by* **spoil,** *many days.34Now when* **they shall fall,** *they shall be helped with a* **little help**:*but many shall cleave to them with flatteries. 35And some of them of understanding* **shall fall,** *to try them, and to purge, and to make them white, even to the time of the end: because it is yet for a time appointed. 36and the King shall do according to his will; and he* **shall exalt himself,** *(the anti-Christ) and* **magnify himself above every god,** *and shall speak marvelous things against the God of gods, and shall prosper till the*

indignation be accomplished: *for that which is determined shall be done. *37Neither shall he regard the God of his fathers, nor the desire of women, nor regard any god: for he shall **magnify himself above all.** *38But in his estate shall he honor the God of fortresses: and a god whom his fathers knew not shall he honor with gold, and silver, and with precious stones, and pleasant things. *39Thus shall he do in the strongest fortresses with **a strange god,** whom he shall acknowledge and increase with glory: and he shall cause them to **rule over many,** and **shall divide the land for gain.**
*40and at the time of the end shall the king of the south push at him: and the king of the north shall come against him like a whirlwind, **and chariots,** and **with horsemen,** and with **many ships;** *41and he shall enter into the countries, and shall **overflow and pass over.** He shall enter also in the glorious land, and many countries shall be overthrown: but these shall escape out of his hand, even Edom, and Moab, and the chief of the children of Ammon *42He shall stretch forth his hand also upon the countries: and the land of **Egypt shall not escape.** *43But he shall have power over the treasures of gold and of silver, and over all the precious things of Egypt: and the **Libyans** and the **Ethiopians shall be at his steps.** *44But tidings out of the east and out of the north shall trouble him: **therefore he shall go forth with great fury to destroy,** and utterly to sweep away many. *45And he shall plant the tabernacles of his palace between the seas in the glorious holy mountain; **yet he shall come to his end, and none shall help him."**

Rev. 16:13-16, Zech. 14:1-4, and *Joel 3.* This will be a collision between East and West.

JESUS WILL RETURN

Jesus will return, intervene, destroy the anti-Christ and reign over the earth.

📖 **Zech. 14:12,9,** *12"And this shall be the plague wherewith the Lord will smite all the people that have fought against*

99

Jerusalem: Their flesh shall consume away while they stand upon their feet, and their eyes shall consume away in their holes, and their tongue shall consume away in their mouth. ⁹*And* **the Lord shall be king over all the earth:** *in that day shall there be one Lord, and his name one.*

📖 **2 Thess. 2:8,** *"And then shall that* **Wicked** *be* **revealed,** *whom* **the Lord shall consume with the spirit of his mouth,** *and shall destroy with brightness of his coming:"*

FINAL SEVEN YEAR WEEK

Out of the current Middle-East talks between Israel, the Palestinians and Arab States,will eventually materialize a compromised, **Interim Agreement.** This will form the basis for the **initiation** of **the final 7 year week** of **Daniel,** under the auspices of the World Order and Anti-Christ. *Daniel 9:27.*

TWO ANTI-CHRISTS

There will be two Anti-Christs. The first,**a forerunner** to the second, in accordance with *Rev. 13.* The first, will incorporate the mind of the great former Empires ; Egypt, Assyria, Babylon, Persia, Greece, and Rome, plus his own thinking. The **Second anti-Christ or false prophet,** will reflect the mind and spirit of the first. However, there will be no lasting peace until the Return of the Prince of Peace.

THE ROMAN EMPIRE
IS
COMING BACK

Chapter Ten

The Roman Empire consisted of **East and West,** represented by **the two iron legs** of man's image in, *Dan. 2.* By 395, the Empire was divided into East and West dimensions. The ten root races of Western and Eastern Europe, are the tribes which overran Europe during the Fourth and Fifth Centuries AD. **The Nations of Continental Europe are descendants of these major races.**

In the West are the Goths, the Gauls, the Franks, the Lombards and the Anglo-Saxons. In the East, the Sythian branch of the Goths or Russians, the Huns, the Slavs, the Greeks and the Turks. These are basically the ten races of the entire world except for the Shemites and Hamites in the Middle East and Africa.

IRON AND CLAY

The feet and the toes of Iron are merely an extension of the legs. Therefore, they are an extension, or continuation of the Iron Roman Empire, branching out into the One World Order.

The clay represents the fragile systems of Democracy and Pluralism. These are also divided into diverse elements of racial or ethnic, religious and political groups mixed with humanism, or seeds of men.

THE ANTI-CHRIST

The coming anti-Christ is to emerge from the people of the revived Roman Empire, even through he himself can be of Jewish descent. He would still be from among the people who destroyed Jerusalem, in 70 AD.

The Prophet Daniel says Messiah was to be cut off, not for himself, but for the sins of the world, *Dan.9:26, Matt. 23:36-39, John 1:29. Then Daniel says , "And the people of the prince that shall come, shall destroy the city and the sanctuary, or temple."* Not the prince but the people of the prince that shall come later. The Roman Empire, under the Roman General Titus, in 70 AD, destroyed Jerusalem and the Jewish Temple.

This specific reference, *"the people of the prince that shall come,"* refers to the Roman people, as they are the ones who destroyed the city. This prince arises later in the end-time for the final seven year week, or week of years, and supports the Israeli Covenant, which includes the Restored Tabernacle Service on the Temple Mount, in an agreement involving the World Order, or Rome, Israel, the Palestinians and Arabs.

Rev.11:1-3, Dan. 9:27. After 3½ years,or in the Middle of the 7 year week, **he** breaks his agreement, **defiles the Tabernacle,** and causes the sacrifice to cease.

Dan. 11:28,30-32, 2 Thess.2:4. True to God's Word and The Prophecy, today we witness the move toward eliminating national borders in Western Europe and the consolidation of Continental Europe, East and West, into the Pan-European Alliance.Soon **a dominant leader will emerge from this alliance,** as the **leading spokesman** of the new order, the revived Roman Empire will forge an alliance with Israel and the Middle-East.

This European alliance will compose a powerful, political and economical force, with Germany as the strongest component. Anti-Semitism is rising there again. Germany has already signed a pact with Russia. Europe is moving toward a common currency. France just voted for political economic integration of Europe. This union is being sought in Europe to offset economic and currency instability. Most leaders in the United States support the union of all of Europe, thinking it will offer a greater market, particularly for US Agricultural exports.

The final state of the revived Roman Empire politically is portrayed as being an Empire which will branch out to the whole world. This order of world-wide dominion is verified in the prophecy of, *Rev.13:7,8.*

Out of the Middle-East Peace talks will emerge the seven year arrangement of , *Dan.9:27.* This will be an interim, or

103

temporary agreement. In this agreement, **Israel will not give away the West Bank.** The West Bank was given to Judah, and **Israel will never be separated from Judah again.** The two will remain one nation, *Ezek. 37:19,22.* Israel will give autonomy to the Palestinians to administrate their daily affairs.We support Israel. However, **the Palestine and Arab peoples will also be blessed,** for they too are children of Abraham.They will not be blessed at Israel's expense, or loss of national security. Remember, the **sons of Jacob will not be consumed.** There will be no permanent peace in the Middle-East until the Return of the Prince of Peace.The Middle-East will be divided into three major segments.

📖 **Isa.19:23-25,** *23"In that day shall there be a highway out of Egypt to Assyria, and the Assyrian shall come into Egypt, and the Egyptian into Assyria, and the Egyptians shall serve with the Assyrians. 24IN THAT DAY SHALL ISRAEL BE THE THIRD WITH EGYPT AND WITH ASSYRIA,even a blessing in the midst of the land; 25Whom the Lord of Hosts shall bless, saying,* **Blessed be Egypt my people, and Assyria, the work of My hands, and Israel mine inheritance."**

THE PRINCE OF PEACE WILL BRING ABOUT THE
JUST AND LASTING SOLUTION.

THE PERSIAN GULF CRISIS

Chapter Eleven

On August 2, 1990, Saddam Hussein of Iraq, in violation of International Law, blatantly and brutally invaded the Sovereign Nation State of Kuwait, his southern neighbor. This was an appalling act to the Western World, and to all peace-loving nations. The action was followed by numerous atrocities, killings, torture and rape, robbery, and kidnapping, perpetrated upon the Kuwaiti people.

The United States then played a major leading role in the formation of a coalition, or multi-national force moving into the Red Sea, the Persian Gulf Region, and particularly into Saudi Arabia. This was a legitimate expediency under International Law; supported by world interest in protecting the rights of sovereign nations; to protect the oil supply in the interest of the International economy; in the interest of United States and Western Security, by the United Nations economic sanctions and embargo resolutions and the right granted by the United Nations to use military force, if necessary, to enforce the embargo, by request from the Kuwaiti and Saudi Governments, in defense of their countries and finally the United Nations Resolution to use force in evicting Iraq from Kuwait.

When Saddam Hussein saw he was in deep trouble, he quickly focused the conflict on Israel, and compared his invasion of Kuwait to the Israel occupation of the West Bank. He did this to gain the support of the Palestinian people and other Arab States in the attempt to also weaken the allied coalition. There was no comparison actually between the invasion of Kuwait and the West Bank occupation, because Kuwait is a Sovereign nation-state, while the West Bank is not, and has never been, in modern

105

times, a Sovereign entity.Saddam also upset the balance of power militarily in the Middle East posing a threat to the stability and security of the region, and to the peace of the world. It was a question of whether the United States and the Coalition should pay in 1991 or pay later. The price later would be higher, giving Saddam more time to build his military machine and to develop ultimately Nuclear Weapons and longer range missiles.

A PANORAMIC VIEW

For now, high tech won the war as far as expelling Iraq from Kuwait. **Isaiah, Jeremiah,** and **Zechariah** envisioned a panoramic view of an Endtime series of **Middle-Eastern wars.** The ultimate fulfillment of these wars were in our time, just prior to the Coming of the Lord, because the prophets, who were watching the events of these nations in their day, watched the drama play out down to our day, or to the very end of these nations.

BATTLE HYMN OF THE AGES

What we are seeing today, is a replay of ancient wars being fought between the national **offspring of their ancestors**. The nations today fight the same wars as their founding fathers. It is **the battle hymn of the ages.** The age old conflict centers on the dispute begun between **Isaac,** Father **of Israel**, and **Ishmaal**, Father **of the Arab Palestinians,** four thousand years ago. The conflict basically is a deep **rooted theological dispute,** involving a geo-political piece of real estate, called **The Promised Land**.

📖 **Zech. 11:1,** states, *"Open thy doors, O Lebanon, that the fire may devour thy cedars. Howl, fir tree: for the cedar is fallen; because the mighty are spoiled; howl, O* *ye oaks of Bashan; for the forest of the vintage is come down."* Since Lebanon opened her doors to the PLO in the 1970's, she has not been the same since. The cities of Lebanon are laid waste. Beirut lies in ruins.In *Isa. 23,* the prophet sees the **waste and destruction of Lebanon** involving the cities of Tyre and Sidon. The ancient name for **Iraq was Babylon.**

Isa. 13:1, the **burden of Babylon,** which Isaiah, the son of Amoz, did see. *Verses 4-6,* "the noise of a multitude in the mountains, like as of a great people, a tumultuous noise of the **kingdoms of nations** gathered together: the Lord of Hosts mustereth the host of the battle. They came from a **far country,** from the **end of heaven,** even the Lord, and the weapons of his indignation, to destroy the whole land. *Howl ye: for the day of the Lord is at hand; it shall come as a destruction,from the Almighty."*

"Kingdoms of Nations" here indicates blocs of nations forming a world order, or a multi - national force. The Hebrew word for *"Nations",* is *goy,* meaning **foreign** or **Gentiles,** like a flight of locusts. *"Far country",* in Hebrew, is *mer-klvawk,* meaning a **remote place,** or a **distant place.**

DAY OF THE LORD IS AT HAND

"End of heaven," in Hebrew, is *Getz,* meaning **extremity, utmost** or the **opposite side.** The opposite of Iraq in the East would be in the West. Thus, these nations involve the United States and the multi-national forces from the Western World, with awesome weapons of indignation. When shall this event occur? What is the time frame? *Isa. 13 verse 6 says, "the Day of the Lord is at hand."* *Verse 9* says, *"behold the day, the day of the Lord cometh with wrath."* **The Day of the Lord** in Bible prophecy, is the key

phrase denoting the Coming of the Lord. The seventh day of the world week. **The thousand year - day** of the Lord's Reign. The Lord's Day, or 7th day.

📖 **2Pet.3:8-10,** [8]*"But, beloved, be not ignorant of this one thing, that one day is with the Lord as a thousand years, and* **a thousand years as one day.** [9]**The Lord is not slack concerning his promise,** *as some men count slackness; but is long-suffering to us-ward, not willing that any should perish, but that all should come to repentance.* [10]*But the day of the Lord will come as a thief in the night; in the which the* **heavens shall pass** *away with a great noise, and the* **elements shall melt** *with fervent heat, the earth also and the* **works that are therein shall be burned up."**

From *Rev. 4:1,* **John saw** things to occur in the future, beyond his own time. He saw in *Rev. 6:17* , **The Great Day of Wrath.**

Thus, the ultimate fulfillment of *Isa. 13,* was to occur just prior to the Day of the Lord. This brings it down to our day in the 20th Century. It definitely involves Iraq. *Isa. 13:10,* depicts t**he sun, moon, and stars being darkened** out in this conflict. The **black smoke from the burning oil wells in Kuwait** set by Saddam **blackened out the sun, moon, and stars over Kuwait** and much of Iraq. The soot, sulfur, or brimstone falls down upon the land, with **black rain coming down** upon the region. The ecology is upset and the chemicals destroyed by allied bombs were reportedly leaked out into the soil, *Isa. 13:20.*

The **Ravenous bird** of the East was raised up, resulting in a catalyst to draw people closer to God, including Israel. *Isa. 46:10-13,* the **Falcon** is in t**he Ravenous bird** family hunting smaller, weaker prey. The **state seal of Iraq** is the **Falcon**.

EDOM TRAVAILED

There was a cry in the Red Sea as, *Edom,* or Saudi Arabia, travailed, and *he flew as an eagle, spreading his wings over Bazrah.* The **symbol of the United States** is the **Eagle,** flying as the screaming eagles over the area.

Jer 49:21-22, "make bright arrows and gather the shields." *Jer 51:11,* "Arrows," here, indicates missiles. Bright or fiery missiles flying over the Middle East. The shields are appropriately applied to Operation Desert Shield, which became a whirlwind in the desert, Desert Storm, *Jer. 51:1. Jer. 50:46,* at the noise of the taking of **Babylon,** the earth is moved, and the cry is heard among the nations." To paraphrase; **at the noise of the taking of Iraq, the earth is moved or changed, and the cry is heard among the nations.**

Twenty four hours after the allied bombing of Baghdad began, I was appearing on TV Channel 21 program "Word Alive", in Louisville, Kentucky. The host Pastor, Rev. Bob Rodgers, turned to me and asked, "Dr. Carman, when will this war be over?" The answer came to me in a flash and I replied, "It will be over by spring, by the first of March." Bob said," that sounds good." By the last of Feb., the war was officially suspended. The reason the war went as smooth as it did is because, the Lord of Hosts "Mustered the Host of the battle,"*Isa. 13:4.*

This war, with the coalition of nations, waged against Babylon (modern Iraq), **was a sign** that the Day of the Lord is near at hand, *Isa. 13:6.*

Russia has an established voice in the region as a partner in the **New World Order.** Iran has also made moves to fill the vacuum left by Iraq in the Persian Gulf, as has Syria with assigned United Nations sponsored troops, under the auspices of the United Nations and **One World Order.** The United States will also maintain a residual military presence in the area, especially from the Navy.

The Kurdish rebels were badly beaten back, and brutally slaughtered and driven from their homes as starving refugees by Saddam's troops. The United States and Western Nations did nothing to give them military support or supplies because they proclaimed they had no authority to do so from the United Nations. This indicates **the United States is forfeiting its sovereignty to a One World Government.**

The World Government prophesied in the scriptures , *Dan. 2:41-43, Rev. 13:8, and Rev. 17-18.* Yet the United States supported the Afghan rebels and the Contras in Central America with arms.

The Israeli - Palestinian conflict will continue with more pressure on Israel to **give up land for peace.** Israel will become more involved in Middle East later, as wars and rumors of war continue in the area. I would not be surprised, if forces from Iran, or associated with Iran, work to topple the Saddam Hussein regime in Iraq. It is written, *"Behold, I will stir up the medes against them* (Iraq or Babylon) *Isa. 13:17.* A repeat, or replay of ancient history as the ultimate fulfillment of *Isa. 13*, as **the Day of the Lord approaches.** The Medes, or media is located in Northwestern Iran. **The Medes are the Modern Kurds**. Shiite Moslems in Iraq are associated with Iran, *Dan.5:28.*

The Kingdoms of Nations mentioned in *Isa. 13:4*, aimed against Iraq, was the beginning of **a World Order.** Not just a nation, but Kingdoms of Nations formed cohesively as a world order in opposition to Iraq, the modern territory of ancient Babylon.

JORDAN

Soon, Jordan will go into turmoil and King Hussein of Jordan will lose power because of the position he took during the Persian Gulf Crisis. *Jer. 49:1-3.* **Concessions eventually will be made by Israel** to make peace with the Arab states and Palestinians. At least an interim, or **temporary agreement,** will be worked out between the Palestinians and Israel **under the World Order.** However, the **West Bank will still remain a part of Israel,** and ultimately Israel will be allowed to place the **Tabernacle of David** on the North Western side of the **Temple Mount in Old Jerusalem.**

There will be **conflict also between Israel and Syria.** Damascus, the Capital city of **Syria, will be totally annihilated.** It will cease to be a city. This is still future, because Damascus, in history, has never ceased to be a city since it became a one. *Isa. 17:1, Jer. 49:23-27.* Israel will also be involved in the future destruction of Iraq, *Isa. 14:25, Mi. 5:5-6.*

111

MYSTERY MAGOG

Chapter Twelve

After the **restoration** of the **Tabernacle,** a **power** from the utmost parts of the **North swarms down** in blitz fashion, with the air cover as of clouds, for an **invasion** of the restored **Land of Israel.** **God will** have actually put hooks into the jaws of this power, leading them into Israel, for what will **become their defeat.** Their waterloo. God is **against Gog** because they have already sponsored five major wars against the seed of Abraham. *Gen. 12:3*, *"And I will bless them that bless thee, and curse him that curseth thee: and in thee shall all families of the earth be blessed."* **God** will also **terminate** their **power** because in attacking Israel, this is a strike against God's plan,relative to Israel.

GOG & MAGOG

Who and **what** is this **Gog and Magog?** This Northern land is under the Chief Prince of Meshech. *"Meshech"*, is a derivative of *Moscow.* The word *"Chief Prince"*, in Hebrew, of which this was originally written, is *"Rosh".* *Rosh* is the feminine form of *"Russia"*, in Hebrew. Josephus, the Historian, who lived prior to the destruction of Jerusalem nearly 2,000 years ago, says in his <u>History of Jewish Antiquities,</u> that the ancient Scythians occupied this territory North of the Black Sea. These were the ancestors of the Russian People.

Magog was the grandson of Noah, and his offspring occupied what is now called Russia. St. Ambrose in De Eiccessu Fratris AD. 378, associates Magog as the **Goths**. In the <u>Jewish Talmud,</u> L.Gensburg says, Magog is the territory of the **White Huns,** or Southern Russia.

The text would read in Hebrew, "set thy face against *Gog* of the land of *Magog*, of *Rosh, Meshech*, and *Tubal"*. *Mesheck* is related to *Muscovy,* or *Moscow.* The word

"Rosh" in Hebrew, means **head, or chief.** The Greek Septuagint translation, also identifies Gog as the **Prince of Rosh.** The German Protestant Hebraist, Gesenius, says that **Gog is** undoubtedly the **Russians.** We also know this to be a fact from the names of the other regions associated with Chief Prince, or Rosh.

"Magog", the land of Gog, meaning, **mountain,** was located in what is called today the **Caucasus, land of the Ancient Scythians.**Josephus, the Historian, said, "**Magog,** or the **Magogites** were called by the Greeks, Scythians. The Scythians believe their ancestors came from Araxes, in Armenia, which is now in the Soviet Union. **Japheth was the father of Magog,** *Gen. 10:1-2.* Those who the Greeks called *"Sarmatians"*, a blend of Medes and Scythians, who settled in the region of the Black Sea and spread out from the Baltic to the Urals. Their offspring now are known as **Tartars, Cassocks, Finns, Kalmuks and Mongols.**

MAGOG - COALITION

In the Hebrew lexicography, Gesenius, identified *"Meshech"* as **Moscow or Muscovy.** He associated Tubal, as Tabalsk, a **part of Russia.** They were to come into Israel from the uttermost parts or extreme North. All these directions are relevant to Israel. **Moscow is to the extreme due North.** Furthermore, the same nations mentioned in **Ezek. 38,** as part of the **Magog Coalition** are **nation's** which have been **armed by** the **Soviet Union** today and are **Hostile toward Israel.**

Persia is the ancient name of Modern **Iran, Ethiopia and Libya.** In *Ezek.38:6,* we have Gomer, and all his hordes, or bands. These people moved westward into what is now Germany. The Jewish Talmud, states that the sons of **Gomer were Germans.** The Soviet Union, in 1990, signed

113

a pact with Germany. Togormah, in the north quarters, is Asia Minor, divided today between **Turkey, Iran and the Soviet Union.**

The actions of Magog are questioned by opposing forces such as **Sheba** and **Dedan** and the **Young Lions of Tarshish.**

📖 **Ezek. 38:13.** *"Sheba, and Dedan, and the merchants of Tarshish, with all **the young lions** thereof, shall say unto thee, **Art thou come to take a spoil?** Hast thou gathered thy company to take a prey, to carry away silver and gold, to take away cattle and goods, **to take a great spoil?"***

Sheba and Dedan are parts of Saudi Arabia. **The "Young Lions of Tarshish"** are the **colonies** founded by the ancient **Phoenician traders** who built the great shipping center of Tarshish, in Europe. This was done prior to the time of Ezekiel. There is evidence that these shippers came to North America, and also the British Isles. The symbol of Great Britain is still the Lion. Notice that **Great Britain**, **The United States,** and **Canada** now have troops together in **Saudi Arabia.** These are **the Young Lions of Tarshish.**

The Magog **invasion will occur** in the latter,or last days of the Gentile Age, **after the Tabernacle has been restored** with the sacrifice. This will be **during a time of peace and safety** brought into Israel, the Middle East, and the World under the anti-Christ. This will therefore occur during the first three and a half years of his seven year rule,or the 70th week of Daniel.

📖 **Ezek. 37:26-28**, 26*"moreover **I will make a covenant** of peace with them; it shall be an everlasting covenant with them: and I will **place them**, and **multiply them***,

114

and will set my sanctuary in the midst of them for evermore. [27]*My tabernacle also shall be with them: yea, I will be their God,* [28]*and they shall be my people. And the heathen shall know that I the Lord* **do sanctify Israel**, *when* **my sanctuary** *shall be in the midst of them* **for evermore."**

📖 **Ezek.38:8,11,** [8]*"After many days thou shalt be visited: in the latter years thou shalt come into the land that is brought back from the sword, and is gathered out of many people, against the mountains of Israel,which have been always waste: but it is brought forth out of the nations, and they shall dwell safely, all of them.* [11]*And thou shalt say, I will go up to the land of unwalled villages;* **I will go to them** *that are at rest, that dwell safely, all of them dwelling without walls, and having* **neither bars nor gates."**

📖 **Dan. 9:27,** *"And he shall* **confirm the covenant** *with many for one week: and in the midst of the week he shall cause the sacrifice and the* **oblation to cease,** *and for the overspreading of abominations* **he shall make it desolate,** *even* **until the consummation,** *and that determined, shall be poured upon the desolate."*

📖 **Dan. 8:25,** *"And through his policy also he shall cause* **craft to prosper** *in his hand; and he shall* **magnify himself in his heart**, *and by peace shall destroy many: he shall also stand up against the Prince of princes;* **but he shall be broken without hand."**

📖 **Rev.13:5,** *"And there was given unto him a mouth speaking great things and blasphemies; and power was* **given unto him to continue forty and two months."**

115

Magog is coming down **in desperation.** Desperation **for food, capital, and natural resources.** They are coming down for the energy resources, the rich minerals of the Dead Sea, the strategic advantages of the Middle East, and the warm water ports of the Indian Ocean.

Only Israel will stand in their way, as was the case during all the great kingdoms of history, in their grab for power and wealth. They will also see the abundance of Gold and Silver recovered with Tabernacle Treasures,*Ezek.38:12-13.*

GOD IS MAGNIFIED

God intervenes and shakes the region. He calls for a sword, **He aids Israel to victory** with an astonishing defeat of the invading confederacy. **God is magnified** before the World with this shocking outcome. *Ezek. 38:23, "Thus will I magnify myself, and sanctify myself; and I will be known in the eyes of many nations, and they shall know that I am the Lord."* The Holy Spirit will be poured out upon Israel. Messiah will no longer hide his face from them. His identity is revealed. *Ezek. 39:28-29, Hos. 5:15.*

There will be some of this war spread to the nations and Isles of the Gentiles. *Ezek. 39:6," And I will send a fire on Magog, and among them that dwell carelessly in the isles: and they shall know that I am the Lord." Gen. 10:5, "By these were the isles of the Gentiles divided in their lands; every one after his tongue, after their families, in their nations."* Magog, the King of the north,will be **reduced in power.**

MAGOG BATTLE IS NOT ARMAGEDDON

The **Magog invasion** of Israel **is not Armageddon. Armageddon will occur much later,** although the wars in the Middle East will be the Genesis and the stirring of the pot of nations **leading to Armageddon.**

WHEN ?

The Magog Battle *Ezek. 38*, occurs near the **beginning** of the **seven year period.** *Dan. 9:27*, **Armageddon** occurs at the **end of the seven years. The Magog Battle** is fought **in the mountains.** Much of **Armageddon** will be **fought on the plains.** Magog will only include specified nations with Russia in the Moslem confederacy, while **Armageddon includes the nations of the World.**

WHO ?

The rule of **anti-Christ,**beyond the **defiling of the Temple,**lasts about three and a half years. At the expiration of that time, **he and his forces** and **all the nations** coming **against Jerusalem** are **destroyed** and **judged by the Returning Christ Jesus.**

📖 **Matt. 24:29-30,** [29]*"Immediately after the tribulation of those days shall the sun be darkened, and the moon shall not give her light, and the stars shall fall from heaven, and the powers of the heavens shall be shaken:*[30]*And then shall appear the sign of the Son of man in heaven: and then shall all the tribes of the earth mourn, and they shall see the* **Son of man coming in the clouds of heaven with power and great glory.** *"*

📖 **Rev. 16:14-16,** [14]*"For they are the spirits of devils, working miracles, which go forth unto the kings of the earth and of the whole world, to gather them to the battle of that great day of God Almighty.* [15]*Behold, I come as a thief. Blessed is he that watcheth, and* *keepeth his garments, lest he walk naked, and they see his shame. ¹⁶And he gathered them together into a place called in the Hebrew tongue, **Armageddon."***

📖 **Zech. 14:3-4,** ³***"Then shall the Lord go forth**, and fight against those nations, as when he fought in the day of battle. ⁴And his feet shall stand in that day upon the Mount of Olives, which is before Jerusalem on the east*, and the Mount of Olives shall cleave in the midst thereof toward the east and toward the west, and there shall be a very great valley; and half of the mountain shall remove toward the north, and half of it toward the south."*

REMNANT FLEES

When the anti-Christ desecrates the Tabernacle by entering it, a Jewish Remnant flees into the wilderness.

📖 **Matt. 24:15,** *"When ye therefore shall see the abomination of desolation, spoken of by Daniel, the Prophet, stand in the Holy Place, (whoso readeth, let him understand:)"*

📖 **Rev. 12:6,** *"And the woman fled into the wilderness, where she hath a place prepared of God, that they should feed her there a thousand two hundred and threescore days."*

The attention of the anti-Christ is distracted from them by bad news from the North and the East. Therefore, **Armageddon will be fought between the anti-Christ and his forces from the West, and the massive armies from the East. An East-West collision of destruction.** A war to take over and solidify power over Jerusalem and Israel. To rule the wealth of the Middle East. The bad news is that

118

the anti-Christ is confronted with 200 million troops coming from the East. These **converging upon the Middle East with awesome destructive force.** *Rev. 16:12-16, Rev.9:14-16, Dan. 11:41-45, Joel 3:2, Zech. 14:3-4.*

JESUS RETURNS
CONSUMES THE ANTI-CHRIST

Jesus will then **return,** and **intervene** to save Israel, and the Earth, and He will **consume** the **anti-Christ** and the armies with the spirit of his mouth, *2 Thess. 2:8, Zech. 14:12.* Jesus and the Saints will then reign over the Earth during an Age of Peace and Justice **for one thousand years.**

📖 **Rev. 20:4,** *"And I saw thrones, and they sat upon them, and judgment was given unto them: and I saw the souls of them that were beheaded for the witness of Jesus, and for the word of God, and which had not worshipped the beast, neither his image, neither had received his mark upon their foreheads, or in their hands; and* **they lived and reigned with Christ a thousand years."**

THE LORD'S HOUSE ESTABLISHED

📖 **Isa. 2:2-4,** *2"it shall come to pass in the last days, that the mountain of the* **Lord's house shall be established** *in the top of the mountains, and shall be exalted above the hills; and all nations shall flow unto it. 3 And many people shall go and say,* **'Come ye, and let us go up to the mountain of the Lord, to the house of the God of Jacob;** *and he will teach us of his ways, and we will walk in his paths: for out of Zion shall go forth the law, and the word of the Lord from Jerusalem. 4* **And he shall judge among the nations,** *and shall*

119

rebuke many people: *and they shall beat their* **swords into plowshares,** *and their spears into pruning hooks: nation shall not lift up sword against nation,* **neither shall they learn war any more."**

HIS GOVERNMENT, HIS PEACE, HIS MILLENNIAL KINGDOM

📖 **Isa. 9:6-7,** [6]*"For unto us a* **child is born, unto us a son is given:** *and* **the government** *shall be upon his shoulder: and his name shall be called* **Wonderful, Counselor, The Mighty God, The Everlasting Father, The Prince of Peace.** [7]*Of the increase of* **His Government** *and* **Peace** *there shall be* **no end, upon the throne of David,** *and upon his kingdom, to order it, and to establish it with judgment and with justice* **from henceforth even forever.** **The zeal of the Lord of Hosts will perform this."**

DESTINY OF AMERICA

Chapter Thirteen

Our Forefathers carved an Empire out of a hidden wilderness and God blessed this nation with prosperity unequaled in the annuals of human history. America was given a **special destiny,** tied to God's plan for the planet.

When the **Pilgrims** came to this new land on the Mayflower, they signed a **covenant** called the **Mayflower Compact.** God was included in this covenant. In route to Massachusetts,Governor John Wintrop, aboard the Arabella proclaimed, *"The God of Israel is among us. We shall be a city set on a hill, that cannot be hid."*

When the Declaration of Independence was signed in 1776, Samuel Adams, the Boston merchant, arose with a voice of emotion, *"we have this day restored the Sovereign to whom alone men ought to be obedient. He reigns in Heaven, and from the rising to the setting sun, may His Kingdom Come."*

EXCEPT THE LORD BUILD THE HOUSE

When the Constitutional Convention was deadlocked in 1787, it looked as through the **Great American Dream** would die within the Philadelphia Hall. Then, Benjamin Franklin arose and said, *" If a sparrow cannot fall to the ground without God's notice, how can an empire arise*

without His aid ?Except the Lord build the House, they labor in vain that build it."
Franklin suggested the delegates **begin the session with prayer** each morning. The deadlock was broken and **there emerged the great Constitution of the United States.**

The first amendment to the US Constitution states, *"Congress shall make no law respecting an establishment of religion, or prohibiting the free exercise thereof."***It did not say Congress shall separate God and Country or be oblivious to the Ten Commandments.** To the contrary, the Constitution itself is built on a system based on the Ten Commandments. The intent of our Forefathers is stated by the convention delegate and recording secretary, James Madison, in the Federalist Papers.

The intent was not to repeat the oppression experienced under the state established Church of England. An establishment,or denomination of religion, versus allegiance to God and religion in general. America became the salad bowl of the world, with a diversity of races and cultures. The crucible of freedom. A nation inspired by **the Great American Dream and the Free Enterprise System,** giving to every person the legal opportunity to be all they can be. **A haven** for the weary and worn from every nation.

Eighty five to ninety percent of all the financial resources to spread the Gospel around the world has come from the United States of America. Certainly, America was destined to play the major role in the end-time missionary endeavor, of *Matt. 24:14. "Blessed is he that blesses the Seed of Abraham," Gen.12:2-3.* The United States has supported Israel, and was the first nation to recognize Israel's Declaration of Independence as a Nation, May 14, 1948.

America The Beautiful was designed by God with a diversity of scenery and people, precious multiple hues and shades, gleaming streams, majestic mountains, plains and valleys, stretching between two great resplendent oceans of blue. America is referred to in the scriptures.

Isa. 13:5, The far country which led the Kingdoms of Nations against Iraq, or the geographical territory of ancient Babylon. *Jer.49:22,* The Eagle which flew over Bozrah during the Persian Gulf War. *Dan. 7:3-4, 3"and four great beasts came up from the sea, diverse one from another. The first was like a Lion and had Eagle's wings; 4I beheld till the wings thereof were plucked, and it was lifted up from the earth, and made stand upon the feet as a man, and a man's heart was given to it. "*

Four great predatory, or empire building kingdoms, rising from the Mediterranean Sea, North, East, South, and West. Great Britain arose at the West end of the sea, symbolized by the Lion and the American Colonies, or Eagle, was plucked away from the Lion in the American Revolution, 1776. Britain was no longer a predatory beast, or empire builder, swallowing up other nations, but had a man's heart instead. *Ezek. 38:13, "The Young Lions, or Colonies of*

123

Tarshish." Established by the Phoenician Sea Traders. The United States, Canada, and the British Isles.

NEW DANGERS

Now, humanism, moral permissiveness, false values, pornography, illegal drugs and violence have invaded our land.

A 300 Billion dollar a year drug business as destroying our populace and much of our youth.

We need a spiritual revival-harvest. Our country has accumulated a 4 Trillion dollar debt. Our public schools, especially in major cities have become Godless environments and war zones, without prayer and <u>Bible</u> reading. *We have had policies without principle, wealth without the word , knowledge without character, worship without sacrifice and churches without commitment. Blessed is the nation whose God is the Lord.*

The nation that forgets God shall be turned into hell, *Ps. 9:17.* **Somebody needs to get back to God's Word**. Someone needs to **preach the Truth,** somebody needs to **remind the world** of a real Heaven and a hot sizzling Hell.

WHAT CAN WE AS CHRISTIANS DO?

✝ **2 Chron. 7:14.** *" If my people, which are called by my Name. shall* **humble** *themselves, and* **pray,** *and* **seek my** *face, and turn from their wicked ways; then will I hear from heaven, and will forgive their sin, and will heal their land."*

✝ **Be committed** to God and the Church.

✝ **Acquire through God's Word,** a reality of the soon **Return of Jesus,** witness **His Saving Grace, His Glory,** and utilize the power of **Praise and Worship to God.**

✝ **Stand up** and **speak** out **for Jesus, for Christian Principles,** and the *Victory will be ours.*

PROGNOSIS FOR AMERICA

America was born out of the 18th Century Great Awakening. Today, just because some people are in sin, does not prevent God from honoring His promises to all those that stand steadfast on God's Word. God told Abraham that he would spare Sodom if he could only find ten righteous people there, because Abraham was faithful to God and was interceding for Sodom. The ultimate judgment will not come upon America, or the world, until after the Rapture of the Saints.

📖 **1Thess. 2:7,** *" For the mystery of iniquity doth already work, only he who now letteth will let, until he be taken out of the way."*

125

📖 **1Thess. 4:16-17,** " [16]*For the Lord himself shall descend from heaven with a shout, with the voice of the archangel, and with the trump of God; and the dead in Christ shall rise first;* [17] *Then we which are alive and remain shall be caught up together with them in the clouds, to meet the Lord in the air; and so shall we ever be with the Lord.* "

📖 **1Thess. 5:2-3,** " [2]*For yourselves now perfectly that the Day of the Lord so cometh as a thief in the night.* [3]*For when they shall say,* **Peace and Safety;** *then sudden destruction cometh upon them, as travail upon a woman with child; and they shall not escape.* "

📖 **1Thess. 5:9,** " *For God hath not appointed us to wrath, but to obtain salvation by our Lord Jesus Christ.* "

📖 **Roman 6:23**, " *For the wages of sin is death; but the* **gift of God is eternal life through Jesus Christ our Lord.** "

God will bless America again and God will judge America, just as he will judge all nations. God will bless America with **a *warning from His End-Time Message.*** He is giving America **space for repentance.** Out of this, is to emerge a sweeping, spiritual revival - harvest. The theme cry is, *"Behold, the Bridegroom cometh, go ye out to meet Him, "* Matt. 25:6.

New doors have been opened for the Gospel of the Kingdom to go out of America into Eastern Europe and the former Soviet Republics. The church must take full advantage of this, while we have the opportunity. The United States will play a major role in the One World Order, and will be a trading partner with the New European Alliance. Will we have **revival or apostasy**? Light on one side, darkness on the other, a **spiritual warfare**. Christ followers and the anti-Christ followers, Humanism and the Stone out of a Mountain. The Rapture of the Saints, and the Tribulation.

SOMEDAY SOON OUR PRINCE WILL COME

When Jesus returns, *the kingdoms of this world will become the Kingdoms of our Lord and of His Christ, Rev. 11:15. He is the mighty God, the wonderful counselor, everlasting Father, and the Prince of Peace, to come with His Divine Government, Isa. 9:6-7.*

The world awaits the **Messiah** who came at the close of the fourth millennia, *to bear a cross,* and will soon come again at the end of the sixth millennia, *to wear a crown*. The Hallelujah Chorus will thunder across the void of space with the most unrestrained praise the universe has ever heard. The selfish propensities of insatiable greed will be expelled, and in its place, eternal tranquillity shall spread like the mist of Eden, and wash upon the shores of the world, because, **Someday Soon Our Prince Will Come.**

127

When the Prince was born in a manger of Bethlehem, nearly two-thousand years ago, wise men came from the East to bring Him gifts. Today, we should offer Him gifts, our lives as a living sacrifice unto the Lord. We should even offer him back our country. *Give America back to God,* this land from sea to shining sea. Then we shall truly *sing with our Prince, " My Country tis of Thee... "*

ASHES OF ADVENTURE

Chapter Fourteen

In 1947, three Bedouin cousins were leading their flocks of sheep and goats through the desert, just to the West of the Dead Sea ,in the Qumran area ,when one of them spied a shiny object in a cave. He threw a stone at the object, and upon further investigation, discovered clay jars in the cave filled with leather scrolls wrapped in linen cloth. The boy did not realize the value of the Scrolls. Late in 1947, the scrolls were brought to Jerusalem by a Syrian Orthodox dealer who had purchased them from the young goat - herder. Four of these seven Scrolls were sold to the Syrian Orthodox Patriarch in Jerusalem. The other three came into the possession of E.L. Sukenik, of Hebrew University. Additional scrolls were found, and these Dead Sea Scrolls, as they were called, turned out to be one of the most significant discoveries in History.①

THE DEAD SEA SCROLLS

The Dead Sea Scrolls are the oldest biblical manuscripts in existence. The Dead Sea Scrolls were copies of the scriptures made **by the Jewish Essenes** between 250 BC. and 70 AD.They were written word for word in comparison with our Old Testament Bibles. These included the Isaiah and Daniel Scrolls and many others, another witness to the validity of the scriptures.

These Scrolls were copied from ancient scriptural manuscripts by the Essenes 250 BC. to 70 AD. They were also contemporary with Jesus. According to both Philo, a first century Jew, and Josephus,Historian. Four thousand Essenes lived in Palestine, approximately 300 lived at Qumran. The life at Qumran matches the way of life taught by the Essenes. Some Essenes began to live at Qumran by at least the reign of John Hyrcanus the Maccabean. The Scrolls are widely linked with a monastic and exiled type of

Essenes. Pliny the Elder, another first century Jew, places one group of Essenes at exactly where Qumran and the eleven caves that housed the Scrolls, are situated.②

THE COPPER SCROLL

One of these scrolls was a <u>Copper Scroll,</u> found in 1952, with writings in ancient Hebrew, describing the location of the Hidden Ashes of the Red Heifer and other Temple Treasures.③

THE ASHES OF THE RED HEIFER

What are the "**Ashes of the Red Heifer**"? In *Numbers 19*, it is recorded that Israel was to offer up a burnt Red Heifer, without blemish, with hyssop, scarlet, and cedar wood. The Ashes were then mixed with running water and sprinkled upon the vessels and the people who had been defiled by contact with a dead body, and for a cleansing offering for sin. The Priest who performed the offering became unclean until evening, the one who was sprinkled became clean, *Num.19:2,5,6,9,10, 17 - 19,21.* This is a **type** and **shadow of the offering of Christ Jesus** for the Church. He became our sin, and was taken down from the cross at evening ,the end of his sacrifice. *2 Cor. 5:21, "For he hath made him to be sin for us, who knew no sin; that we might be made the righteousness of God in him." Eph. 5:25, "Husbands, love your wives, even as Christ also loved the Church, and gave Himself for it."* **The Church is now cleansed by the washing of water by the word.**

HYSSOP

They gave Jesus hyssop upon the cross, and he was clothed in scarlet. *St. John 19:28, "After this, Jesus knowing that all things were now accomplished; that the scripture might be fulfilled; saith, "I thirst."*

Hyssop grows in Southern Israel and was used to make soap or a cleanser. These are mere **"types" of the cleansing blood of Jesus,** just as the Passover lamb, with the hyssop grass mixed in its blood sprinkled on the doorposts of the houses of Israel.

📖   **St. John 1:29,** *"The next day, John seeth Jesus coming unto him, and saith, 'Behold the Lamb of God, which taketh away the sin of the world."*

The Red Heifer, according to Rabbinical literature, was to be at least three years old, but less than four. The ministry of Jesus was three and one half years.④

JESUS' MINISTRY
THREE AND ONE HALF YEARS

The **Red Heifer** was the most unique offering in Israel. First, it was to be **offered** outside the camp, or **outside the city.** **Jesus**, too, was **offered outside the city**, **bearing our reproach.** *Heb.13:12-13.* Secondly, **it had to be a female**, or a heifer. The other offerings could be either male or female.

Thirty shekels of silver was the **price** of the redemption of a **female** or a slave. Fifty shekels for a male, *Lev. 27:4.* Everyday the Jews put silver into the Temple Treasury for the offering of the Para Aduma, or Red Heifer. **Jesus was crucified for thirty shekels of silver to redeem a woman, the Church, the bride of Jesus Christ.**

📖 **Eph. 5:25-33,** 25*"Husbands, love your wives, even as Christ also loved the Church, and gave Himself for it;*

26that he might sanctify and cleanse it with the washing of water by the Word; 27that he might present it to himself a glorious Church, not having spot, or wrinkle, or any such thing; but that it should be holy and without blemish. 28So ought men to love their wives as their own bodies. He that loveth his wife loveth himself.29For no man ever yet hated his own flesh; but nourisheth and cherisheth it, even as the Lord the Church: 30for we are members of his body, of his flesh, and of his bones. 31For this cause shall a man leave his father and mother, and shall be joined unto his wife, and they two shall be one flesh.32This is a great mystery: but I speak concerning Christ and the church.33Nevertheless, let every one of you in particular so love his wife even as himself; and the wife, see that she reverence her husband."

He also freed us from the slavery of sin. Judas was paid from the redemption money of the Temple Treasury. *Matt. 26:14-15, "Then one of the twelve, called Judas Iscariot, went unto the chief priests, and said unto them, what will ye give me, and I will deliver him unto you? And they covenanted with him for thirty pieces of silver."*

Hebrews 9:13, reveals **two propositions. First**, that the sprinkling of the **ashes** did sanctify for the **purifying of the flesh;** and **second**, it was a **type of the offering up of Jesus Christ.** The Church is sanctified and cleansed by the offering of Jesus Christ and His precious blood.

BLOOD BOUGHT BRIDE

The Lord God took a rib from the side of the **first man, Adam,** and made a **woman from the rib.** She became **Adam's wife**. Water and blood came from the side of the **second man Adam, Jesus Christ.** He takes us **through**

the water and the blood and we become the bride of the second man Adam, Jesus Christ.

📖 **Gen. 2:21-24,** ²¹*"And the Lord God caused a deep sleep to fall upon Adam, and he slept: and he took one of his ribs, and closed up the flesh instead thereof;*²² *And the rib, which the Lord God had taken from man, made He a woman, and brought her unto the man.* ²³ *And Adam said, This is now bone of my bones, and flesh of my flesh: she shall be called Woman, because she was taken out of Man.*²⁴*Therefore shall a man leave his father and his mother, and shall cleave unto his wife; and they shall be one flesh."*

📖 **St. John 19:34,** *"But one of the soldiers with a spear, pierced his side, and forthwith came there out blood and water."*

📖 **Cor. 15:45,47,** *"*⁴⁵*And so it is written, The first man, Adam, was made a living soul; the last Adam was made a quickening spirit.* ⁴⁷***The first man is of the earth, earthy: the second man is the Lord from heaven."***

PEARL OF GREAT PRICE

Jesus refers to the "**pearl of great price**", *Matt. 13;45-46.* Where do pearls come from? From the **wounded** side of an **oyster.** The side of the oyster is cut, a secretion comes out and forms into a pearl. The side of Jesus was wounded, water and blood came out. **We are taken through the water and blood and form into a pearl,bought with a price.**

📖 **1Cor. 6:19-20,** ¹⁹*"What? Know ye not that your body is the temple of the Holy Ghost which is in you, which ye have of God, and ye are not your own?*

^{20}***For ye are bought with a price: therefore glorify God** in your body, and in your spirit, which are God's."*

GRAFTED IN

We, as **Gentiles,** were as a branch **grafted into a good olive tree through Jesus Christ,** *Rom. 11:24; Gal. 3:29.* To graft a branch into a tree, the side of the tree must be cut or wounded. The branch is grafted in. If the graft is alive the **third day, the graft was a success.** Jesus was alive the **third day forever more, and we in Him.** He is the vine. *St. John 15;1, Rev. 1:18.*

THE PERPETUAL OFFERING

The method of offering the Red Heifer was to kill and burn the Heifer, throwing the scarlet, hyssop, and cedar stick onto the burning red heifer.Then use the ashes in running, or spring water, for the sprinkling. Only a pinch sufficed. The ashes left over were kept in a clay vessel, inside a copper container called a *Kalal*, or pitcher, in English.

The **ashes left over and kept,** were brought out at the next offering of a red heifer, and **the clay vessel** with the ashes, were set on the red heifer and the whole thing burned together. In this manner, the **new ashes were mixed in and added to the old ashes. This locked the offerings and the ashes together in an unbroken, continuous or successive offering.** This made the offering of Moses a **Perpetual Statute. "***Perpetual***"** meaning, **continuous, unbroken, and unceasing.** Just as the anointing oil of *Ex. 30:31*, was to be used throughout all of Israel's generations. This was a perpetual offering, or statute.*Numbers 19:21,* there would always be some of the ashes from Moses mixed in. **One** Red Heifer was offered in the time of Moses, the

134

second in the time of Ezra when the Temple was rebuilt, and **five** were offered since then. **The last one** was offered just before the destruction of Jerusalem, 70 AD., according to Josephus, History of Jewish Wars, Book 6, Chapter Six. **Seven heifers in all have been offered.** This is fitting, because **seven is a complete number in the Bible,** and the basis for the Jewish Sabbatical System. After the time of Solomon's Temple, the Red Heifer was offered upon the Mount of Olives. The Heifer was offered in line and on the same level of the Eastern Gate. ⑤

THE EASTERN GATE

The head of the Red Heifer pointed directly toward the Eastern Gate in the offering.

The Essenes were a religious sect of the Jews that had split away from the Pharisees, believing the Pharisees were corrupt and defiled. Saying and doing not. The Essenes began to copy and compile the Old Testament Scriptures during the First and Second Centuries BC., at a place called Qumran. Qumran goes back to at least the Ninth Century BC. These copies of the Scriptures and Temple practices are called "The Dead Sea Scrolls". They began to be found in 1947, just before the restoration of the nation of Israel. This was no accident. Knowledge from the Dead Sea Scrolls was necessary for the complete restoration of the kingdom to Israel regarding the ashes, and other temple treasures. The Essenes dwelling place was located in the Judean Desert, of the Valley of Achor, *Hos.2:15.*

TRUE HIGH PRIESTS EXILED

Beginning with King David, the **High Priests of Israel, were the Sons of Zadok.** This lasted until 175 BC. when the Maccabean Hasmonian lineage replaced the Sons of

Zadok. **The true High Priests from Zadok were exiled,** some to Egypt and others to the Essene Community of Qumran. In 37 BC., Herod the Great, an Edomite from the lineage of Esau, was appointed by the Romans as their puppet King of Judea.

He replaced the **Hasmonean High Priest** with his own pals, who then became the **illegitimate High Priests of Israel.** We learn much of this from the <u>Damascus Document</u>. During the time of Herod the Great, the Essenes and the Sons of Zadok lived at Qumran, Also, John the Baptist was in this same area. Qumran was located in the Judean Desert.

The Qumran Essenes regarded the Temple at Jerusalem as polluted and **its priesthood defiled.** They taught that in the end of days the world would be purged of evil, and a new Temple would be built. **The Qumran Community were led by true Priests, the Sons of Zadok.** Archeology confirms that the Essene Community of Qumran was founded in the Middle of the Second Century BC. Prominent among the Essenes at this early stage were the Priests, or Sons of Zadok. This is prevalent in their writings.⑥

Jesus was taken into Egypt for refuge from Herod. John went into the Judean Desert. *Luke 1:80, Matt. 3:1, Matt. 11:7.* It is written that many believed on Jesus in that same region, *St. John 10:42.* The Sons of Zadok were restricted to the Judean Desert, still without access to the Temple at Jerusalem.⑦

ZEALOT'S REVOLT

Then, the **Zealots** from Galilee, under the leadership of John of Giscola, rose up in **revolt against** the **Romans** and **took**

possession of Jerusalem in early November, 67 AD. They **elected a High Priest from the Sons of Zadok,** one **Pinhas of Habta** (67-70 AD.) **the last High Priest of Israel.**⑧

Josephus, the Jewish Historian, was a living eyewitness. The Romans were temporarily expelled from Jerusalem. *Rom. 10:2,* The Zealots and the Essenes in that generation had one thing in common: their dislike for the Romans and their puppet rulers at Jerusalem. The revolt, therefore, gave the **Zadok High Priest and the Essenes temporary access to the Temple at Jerusalem.** However, they knew Rome would return and destroy the Temple. This had been prophesied by both the Essenes and by John the Baptist as the wrath to come, *Matt. 3.* Therefore, they hid the Temple Vessels and the Ashes of the Red Heifer, and the Flask of Anointing Oil. Book of Exodus - Midrash.

Some of these ashes went all the way back to Moses. They knew that one day the Tabernacle would be restored on the Temple Mount and those ashes in the Kalal would be required to cleanse both the Mount and the people, and to resume the Temple service with the old and new ashes.

The Essenes and Zealots made false copies of Temple vessels to mislead the Romans. The Romans thought they were taking the real vessels back to Rome. This is indicated in Josephus' History of Jewish Wars, Book 7, Chapter 6, which says the candlestick carried in the triumphal parade of the Roman General Titus, was not thoroughly like that which was used in the Temple. Josephus says these things taken by the Romans did not agree with **Moses' descriptions,**

📖 **Ex. 25:31-36,** *"31And thou shalt make a candlestick of pure gold; of beaten work shall the candlestick be made: its shaft, and its branches, its bowls, its knobs, and its flowers, shall be of the same. 32And six branches shall come out of the sides of it; three branches of the candlestick out of the one side, and three branches of the candlestick out of the other side: 33Three bowls made like unto almonds in the other branch. with a knob and a flower in one branch; and three bowls made like almonds, with their knops and a flower; So in the six branches that proceed out of the candlestick 34and in the candlestick shall be four bowls made like unto almonds, with their knops and their flowers. 35And there shall be a knop under two branches of the same , and a knop under two branches of the same, and a knop under two branches of the same, according to the six branches that proceed out of the candlestick.36Their knops and their branches shall be of the same: all it shall be one beaten work of pure gold."*

Josephus was indeed an eyewitness of all these things. The Essenes had access to the Temple through the gate of the Essenes. Josephus' History of Jewish Wars, Book 5, Chapter 4. The scripture says the **Tabernacle of David will be raised up**, not another tabernacle. Raised up as in days of old. This is an all inclusive statement. It includes the contents pertaining to the Tabernacle, or the composition of the Tabernacle or as it was in days of old.

These original vessels, that were part of the Tabernacle, **were required for the original Tabernacle to be raised up**. Just as a body is raised from the dead, and it would have all the parts, that make it a body, as it was before. **Such was a "type" of Tabernacle of the Body of Jesus, the Greater Tabernacle, which arose on the third day.**

138

The Roman soldiers paraded through the streets of Rome with these vessels, such as the Menorah, to celebrate their victory over Israel. Titus of Rome made an arch in Rome with the vessels sculptured on it. It is called the "Arch of Titus," and still stands in Rome to this day.

THREE PORTIONS OF ASHES

The Ashes of the Red Heifer were divided and hidden in the three portions: one in the **Temple courtyard,** one on the **Mount of Olives,** and **one** in the **Priest's Quarters.**⑨

The true priests of Israel, the Sons of Zadok, were dwelling at Qumran, in the Valley of Achor. Therefore, a portion of the Ashes should be hidden there with the help of the Zealots and the Essenes. The Copper Scroll, a Dead Sea Scroll found in 1952, lists the hiding of 61 Temple Treasures, and gold and silver, including the Kalal of the Ashes of the Red Heifer. The Scroll describes the location in the Qumran area and another master copy of The Copper Scroll, giving an inventory and explanation of all the treasury. There are at least three other alternative sites of the hidden ashes, other than Qumran where they could be found, according to authentic Jewish writings.

All things will be restored pertaining to the Kingdom of Israel according to *Acts 3:12,20-21.* Since 1952, the Copper Scroll was translated from Hebrew to English by John Allegro and J.T. Milik. The search is on for the ashes and other hidden treasures.

I first became involved with various teams in the early 1980's , I have also worked in conjunction with Hebrew University. I have worked with Gary Collette and Jerusalem Ministries International. This project is a real life Indiana Jones treasure project.When the ashes, Scrolls, and other treasures are found, they will be turned over to certain Rabbis and the Kohenite Priesthood in Jerusalem.

The Ark of the Covenant and the Tabernacle of David cannot be brought out and repitched on the Temple Mount until the ashes have been found for the cleansing of the Temple Mount. The Temple Mount has been touched by dead bodies, *Num. 19.* How do we know the ashes of Moses must be found? First, we know according to Jewish sacrificial laws, that the ashes must be found for the resumption of the Temple service. It is a **perpetual sacrifice,** never ending. To go out and acquire another red heifer would be starting all over. It would not be the perpetual offering that began with Moses. The Mishna Torah confirms this. The Midrash Book of Numbers confirms this. The Jewish Halakhah confirms this. The 19th Chapter of Numbers with the word "perpetual" confirms this. In fact, this is why they kept the leftover ashes in the first place.

WILL THE SACRIFICE BE RESTORED?

This is why they hid the ashes in 70 AD. and were very careful to protect that hiding in the riddle of the Copper Scroll. Will the sacrifice be restored? *Dan.9:27*, states the anti-Christ will cause it to cease. How can it be ceased, if it was never begun? *Rev. 11:1-3*, portrays a restored Temple, or Tabernacle,to house the golden altar (The Altar was hidden with the Ark according to 2 Maccabees 2) in the final 7 years, or 70th week of Daniel. Ezekiel writes very clearly of the restored Priesthood of the Sons of Zadok in a temple with dimensions which have never existed in history. Therefore it is future. *Ezek. 44:15, Ezek. 46:13-15.* This is for a **memorial** in **sacrifices as** our **communion**, **not** for **salvation**.

The Ashes of the Red Heifer are the only offering that could bring purification from the touching of dead bodies, according to the Jewish <u>Torah.</u>

If it were not done according to the Jewish <u>Torah</u>, there would be no significance, or reason for doing it at all. Whether we believe in this offering or not is irrelevant. The Jewish people do, and will not go up to the Mount unless this is accomplished. Yet, *Amos 9:11*, will be fulfilled. From 70 AD., the Temple Mount has been defiled. Therefore, it must be cleansed for Jewish recognition in accordance with *Num. 19:11-17*, in order to be <u>Torah</u> pure.

Rabbi Ben Zion Alkalai wrote, "The Western Wall is endowed with a special sanctity as, indeed, Marmonides, the Jewish Rabbi, wrote in the 12th Century AD., "Therefore it is permissible to offer all the sacrifices although the Temple no longer exists. Unfortunately, there are certain prerequisites lacking, and so we cannot bring sacrifices. For example, we are all afflicted with ritual impurity from touching the dead and we do not have the Ashes of the Red Heifer which are needed to effect purification." **The <u>Halakhah</u> rules that nowadays Jews cannot enter the Temple Mount without the Ashes of Para Adumah.**⑩

PURIFICATION OF MOUNT AND PEOPLE

If the Jews could start over now with another Red Heifer, they could have done so all along and would not have had to meticulously keep and preserve the leftover ashes each time. Nor would they have had to go to such great lengths to have hidden and coded the ashes left in 70 AD.

If Israel begins with another Red Heifer, what ashes will they mix the new ashes with? They must have the ashes of the other seven heifers, to mix with, to continue the perpetual statute. Just as the Red Heifer's Head was pointed toward the Eastern Gate From the Mount of Olives, so Jesus the Prince of Peace will stand on the Mount of Olives and head for the Eastern Gate. Seven heifers were complete and we are complete in Christ.

A NEW DAY

📖 **Zech. 14:4,** *"And His feet shall stand in that day upon the Mount of Olives, which is before Jerusalem on the east, and the Mount of Olives shall cleave in the midst thereof toward the east and toward the west, and there shall be a very great valley; and half of the mountain shall remove toward the north, and half of it toward the south."*

📖 **Ezek. 44:1-3,** [1]*"Then he brought me back the way of the gate of the outward sanctuary which looketh toward the east: and it was shut.* [2]*Then said the Lord unto me; this gate shall be shut, it shall not be opened, and no man shall enter in by it; because the Lord, the God of Israel, hath entered in by it, therefore it shall be shut.* [3]*It is for the **Prince;** the Prince, He shall sit in it to eat bread before the Lord; **He shall enter by the way of the porch of that gate, and shall go out by the way of the same.**"*

Isa. 9:7, THE INCREASE OF HIS GOVERNMENT AND PEACE THERE SHALL BE NO END.

Jesus will walk triumphantly toward and through the Eastern Gate, which will open for Him. He will then stand in victory, facing the literal Tabernacle on the Temple Mount, cleansed according to Jewish law by the recovered ashes of the Seven Heifers. Actually Jesus and the Church will be the Eighth Red Heifer without Spot or Blemish. When asking a

Rabbi in Israel if it is necessary to find the old ashes for the restoration of the Tabernacle, he may or may not answer yes, depending on who he is. But rephrase your question and ask him what Israel and the Jewish people would do if tomorrow the original ashes were found, and then hear his reply. Some will say what difference does it make in God's sight whether or not the Temple Mount is cleansed for the restoring of the Tabernacle on the Mount. My answer is does not Jesus refer to the defilement of the Temple on the Mount by the anti-Christ, as an abomination, *Matt.24:15 , 2 Thess. 2:4.*

What does the ashes of the Red Heifer have to do with Salvation? What has the restoration of the Jewish Tabernacle or the Ark of the Covenant to do with Salvation? The answer to these questions is "nothing." Jesus brought salvation nearly 2,000 years ago. But can we also ask the question, What does the re-establishment of the nation of Israel or the restoration of Jerusalem have to do with Salvation? These too are only natural and material things. But they are all significant as Bible Prophecy, fulfillment and signs pointing to the Coming of Christ Jesus.

These are also a schoolmaster to bring Israel to Christ, *Gal. 3:24, Col. 2:17, Heb. 9:23-24, Heb. 10:1.* The ordinances themselves were never intended for Gentiles, *Num. 19:2.* The Ashes of the Red Heifer could be found in any one of the three hiding places mentioned or in another undisclosed place in the Jerusalem area.

THE HEBREW RENAISSANCE

Chapter Fifteen

The Hebrew prophets had spoken of the restitution of all things pertaining to the kingdom of Israel. *Acts 3:12,20,21.* The Tabernacle was prophesied by Ezekiel, Amos, Hosea, and others to be restored.

The Ephod with the Urim and Thummim stones functioned only with the Ark of the Covenant, the Menorah, and the Seven Golden Candlesticks.

📖 **Hos. 3:4-5,** *4"For the children of Israel* **shall** *abide* **many days** *without* **a king,** *and without a prince, and without a sacrifice, and without an image, and without an ephod, and without teraphim:* *5Afterward* *shall the* **children of Israel return,** *and seek the Lord their God, and David, their King; and* **shall fear the Lord and His goodness in the latter days."**

📖 **Ezek. 37:26-28,** *26"Moreover, I will make a* **covenant of peace** *with them; it shall be an everlasting covenant with them: and I will place them, and multiply them, and will set* **My Sanctuary** *in* **the midst of them** *for evermore.* *27My* **tabernacle also shall be with them:** *yea, I will be their God, and they shall be My people.* *28And the heathen shall know that I,* **the Lord,** *do* **sanctify Israel,** *when My sanctuary shall be in the midst of them for evermore."*

📖 **Amos 9:11,** *"In that day will I raise up the* **Tabernacle of David** *that is fallen, and close up the breaches thereof; and I will raise up his ruins, and I will build it as in the days of old:"*

📖 **Exodus 28:29-30,** *29"And Aaron shall bear the names of the children of Israel in the breastplate of judgment*

upon his heart, when he goeth in unto the holy place, for a memorial before the Lord continually.
30and thou shalt put in the breastplate of judgment, the Urim and the Thummim; and they shall be upon Aaron's heart, when he goeth in before the Lord: and Aaron shall bear the judgment of the children of Israel upon his heart before the Lord continually."

RAISE UP TABERNACLE OF DAVID

Let us analyze *Amos 9:11* again. "In that day will I raise up the Tabernacle of David that is fallen, and close up the breaches thereof; and I will raise up his ruins, and I will build it as in the days of old." This is an all inclusive statement by the Prophet that **everything explicitly in the Tabernacle, or pertaining to the functioning of the Tabernacle, would be restored.** This was to occur in the context of Amos, Chapter Nine, in the day when Israel has been gathered back from the captivity of the nations into their own original land. *Amos 9:15,* **To raise up the Tabernacle of David is not to construct a "new" Tabernacle.**

RAUOCH HAKODESH
PRESENCE OF GOD

The Tabernacle, a type of the body of Jesus, is to be raised up as the body of Jesus was to be raised up, with the life of God in it. Therefore, **the presence of God, will be in the Tabernacle** and the **Ark of the Covenant as it was in days of old.** *St. John 1:1,14,* [1]*"In the beginning was the Word, and the Word was with God, and the Word was God.* [14]*And the Word was made flesh, and dwelt among us, and we beheld His glory, the glory as of the only begotten of the Father, full of grace and truth." Heb. 9:11, "But Christ being come a high priest of good things to come, by a*

145

greater and more perfect tabernacle, not made with hands, that is to say, not of this building;" **The Rauoch Hakodesh Presence of God** was **in the Holy of Holies** in days of old, and so it **will be again.**

THE TABERNACLE TENT RAISED
THE TEMPLE BUILT

The Tabernacle was hidden, or buried, as if it were a body. Therefore, the language in *Amos 9:11*, **"His"**, or in the masculine gender. Just as **David pitched the Tabernacle** first, and then **the more elaborate Temple was constructed later by Solomon, so it will be again.**

First the **Tabernacle Tent,** and **later the Temple** described by Ezekiel will be built by Messiah.①First,the Tabernacle of David will be raised and functioning as in days of old. A full restoration. **A complete Hebrew Renaissance.** While the Church is the Temple of the Lord, and Jesus is the greater and more perfect Tabernacle, this scripture in *Amos 9:11,* is related directly to the **literal Tabernacle of David,** just as the other Old Testament scriptures are pointing directly to Israel. For in days of old,or in the days of David, the Tabernacle was literal.

📖 **1Cor. 3:17,** *"If any man defile the Temple of God, him shall God destroy; for the Temple of God is Holy, which Temple ye are."*

📖 **1Peter 2:5,** *"Ye also, as lively stones, are built up a spiritual house, a holy priesthood, to offer up spiritual sacrifices, acceptable to God by Jesus Christ."*

📖 **Eph. 2:20-22**, [20]*And are built upon the foundation of the apostles and prophets, Jesus Christ himself being the chief corner stone;* [21]*in whom all the building fitly* *framed together groweth unto a holy temple in the Lord:* ²²*in whom ye also are builded together for a habitation of God through the Spirit."*

How was the Tabernacle in days of old? It was a **literal tent** made of animal skins. It was a functioning **Tabernacle with the Ark of the Covenant, filled with the presence of God, overshadowed by the visible Cloud of Glory,** and it was pitched upon Mount Moriah, the Temple Mount. All of this **will be raised up as in days of old,** the Tabernacle body and its organs.

The Ark, the Menorah, the Ephod, Urim and Thummim stones, Shewbread Table of Gold, and the Golden Altar of Incense. A resurrected Tabernacle body. *Ex. 25. Lev, 9:23,* "And Moses and Aaron went into the Tabernacle of the congregation, and came out, and blessed the people: and the glory of the Lord appeared unto all the people."This is confirmed in our New Testament, *Acts 15:14-17.* This is James quoting from *Amos 9:11.*

📖 **Acts 15:14-17,**¹⁴*"Simeon hath declared how God at the first did visit the Gentiles, to take out of them a people for His name.* ¹⁵*And to this agree the words of the prophets; as it is written.* ¹⁶*After this I will return, and will build again the Tabernacle of David,* **a tent pitched** *which is fallen down* **the Tabernacle that fell is the one restored** *and I will build again the ruins thereof, and I will set it up.* ¹⁷**That the residue of men***, might seek after the Lord, and* **all the Gentiles***, upon whom My name is called, saith the Lord, who doeth all these things."*

147

The raising up of the Tabernacle after He has called a people out of the gentiles for His name. This eliminates the possibility that *Amos 9:11* was fulfilled somewhere back in Old Testament days. Rather, it is fulfilled at the close of Gentile times. The Lord has been taking a people out from the Gentiles for His name. Then He says after this, the Tabernacle will be lifted up. **He has visited these Gentiles**, or returned to them, **to use representatives from them in finding the treasures or raising up the desolation's of Israel,** so **His name can be re-established in Jerusalem.** *Ezek. 36:22.* In *Acts 15,* He visited the gentiles, because the prophets said, *"after this I will return, and **will build again the Tabernacle of David."*** As a result, the **residue of men might seek after the Lord.**

REVIVAL

Therefore, the restoration of the Tabernacle will generate a great world-wide revival, or seeking after God. Not because Gentiles are participating in the Tabernacle functioning or service, but because **it is a sign and a demonstration of God's Glory.** The Tabernacle will be fixed as in days of old.

CLOUD OF GLORY

In days of old, a visible Cloud of Glory hovered over the Tabernacle and even the outside congregation could see it. *Lev. 9:23,* supernatural functions occur. **This phenomena will occur again** and representatives, even leaders of nations, will behold it and seek after God.

📖 **Ps. 102:13-15,** [13]*"thou shalt arise, and have mercy upon Zion: for the time to favor her, yea, the set time, is come. [14]For thy servants take pleasure in her stones, and favor the dust thereof. [15]So the **heathen shall fear*** *the name of the lord, and all the kings of the earth thy glory."*

SPIRITUAL COUNTERPART

This is important to us **Christians** as we function as **the spiritual counterpart of the literal tabernacle. It is important to us as a sign.** In playing a role in helping raise up these former desolation's, we will have dialogue and use these restorations to **relate the Messiah to Israel**, and as a leverage to **witness to the Gentile world**, carrying over through the 144,000 Jewish witnesses and even into the Millennial Age. God will take away Israel's heart of stone and give them a new heart with His Spirit, as the final phase of their Renaissance. **Their spiritual regeneration.**

FULFILLMENT OF BIBLE PROPHECY

📖 **Ezek. 36:26-27,** *"A new heart also will I give you, and a new spirit will I put within you: and I will take away the stony heart out of your flesh, and I will give you a heart of flesh. And I will put My Spirit within you, and cause you to walk in My Statutes, and ye shall keep My Judgments, and do them."*

The restoration of the literal tabernacle does not bring salvation to the Jews. Jesus brought that almost 2,000 years ago. But **it is a sign.** It will be a fulfillment of Bible prophecy.

These things in Israel's affliction will also serve as a schoolmaster to bring Israel to the Messiah. *Gal. 3:24.* If you said to me, "my car has been restored", it would mean the whole car had been restored to functioning order steering wheel, transmission, and all of the parts. **The word**

149

"Tabernacle" being restored means all the parts that made it "the Tabernacle" are restored.

NATIONS ROUND ABOUT WILL KNOW THAT GOD IS GOD, AND THAT HE IS THE GOD OF ABRAHAM, ISAAC, AND JACOB. THE SHIKINAH GLORY WILL APPEAR. CHARIOTS OF FIRE WILL ROLL IN THE HEAVENS AND THE PROPHETS WILL RETURN.

THIS IS THE GREAT HEBREW RENAISSANCE!

TABERNACLE ON THE MOUNT

Chapter Sixteen

On the **South side** of the Temple Mount, Mount Moriah, gleaming predominantly over Jerusalem, sets the Moslem **Dome of the Rock**. Underneath the golden dome, decorated in mosaics, rests the huge rock sacred to Islam. The Islamic religion claims this is the rock on which Abraham was going to offer Isaac, and from this rock, they say, their founder, Mohammed, ascended into heaven. This exquisite structure was built here by the Moslems, after conquering Jerusalem, about 691 AD. Until recently, it was thought by most, that the original Jewish Temple had also stood on the same site as the Dome, prior to its destruction by the Romans, in 70 AD. Most of us believed the Dome of the Rock would have to be destroyed, before the Temple could be restructured, perhaps in Armageddon. Upon closer analysis, we learn that the Templars, an order of Knights from Europe during the time of the Crusades, started the theory of the Jewish Temple location on the Moslem Dome site. This was an assumption on their part.

Earlier in the 20th Century, Rabbi Schlomo Goren, in Israel, wrote a thesis proposing an alternative site for the Temple. Rabbi Goren said the **original Temple** was not located on the Dome site, but rather **on the northern side of the Temple Mount**. Later, he would become the Chief Rabbi of Israel. Today, Rabbi Goren has opened an office across the street from the western wall of old Jerusalem, for the purpose of the re-establishment of the Jewish Tabernacle and the restoration of all things pertaining to Israel's National Religious Service. In recent years, Dr. Asher Kaufman, Physicist at Hebrew University in Jerusalem, has researched and made remarkable discoveries related to the true location of the original Jewish Temple.①

151

TRUE LOCATION OF THE TEMPLE

Dr. Kaufman points out the fact that the entrance of the Temple faced eastward, toward the rising of the sun, *Ezek. 8:16*. According to Dr. Kaufman's calculations, the Temple was located about 330 feet (100 meters) to the northwest of the Dome of the Rock, on the Temple Mount, opposite the Eastern Gate. Josephus, the Jewish Historian, was an eye witness of Jerusalem before it was destroyed. In his writings, and from other sources such as the <u>Mishnah Torah</u>, we learn that Dr. Kaufman's findings are accurate. Josephus' <u>History of the Jewish Wars,</u> Book 6, Chapter 5, states that the **entrance to the Jewish Temple was in line with the Eastern Gate of the Eastern Wall of Jerusalem**. It is very obvious from reading *Ezekiel 40-44*, that the **Restored Temple** in the millennial, described by Ezekiel, will be to the **North Side of the Temple Mount with its entrance in line with the Eastern Gate!** *Ezekiel 40:6, 41:1, 42:20*. The profane place, or outer court, is to the opposite side, *Rev. 11:1-3, Ezekiel 43:1-7*. Here, the Lord explains the house, or Temple's entrance, lines up with the Eastern Gate, *Ezekiel 44:1*. The Priesthood of the Sons of Zadok shall be restored, *Ezekiel 44:15-16*.

The <u>Mishnah</u> (Middat 2:1) was **codified** in its present form about **200 AD**. Its contents were composed and transmitted orally from an earlier period, giving the impression that here is the portrayal of an eyewitness. **The Second Temple is described in great detail and in a fairly systematic fashion.** The <u>Mishnah</u> states that the greater part of the outer court, *Har Habbaifit*, was on the **south, the next greater part the east, next on the south, and the smallest part, on the west.** This description in the <u>Mishnah</u> makes it difficult to locate the Holy of Holies at the Dome of the Rock site.

THE EASTERN GATE

Dr. Asher Kaufman, from Hebrew University, began his research survey of the Temple in 1967, after Jerusalem was re-united. He personally pointed out various features of the Temple Mount area to Mr. Shanks, of <u>Biblical Archeology Magazine</u>. Mr. Shanks took photographs of a rock cutting,or a line of grass, perhaps indicating a buried wall. Dr. Kaufman states, **"The Second Temple, as well as Soloman's Temple before it, faced East; that is, it was entered from the East.** The only clearly visible entrance to the Temple Mount from the East is through the Golden Gate. **This is the Eastern Gate through which the Messiah will pass when The Great Day comes.** The Midpoint of the Golden Gate is located about 348 feet (106 meters) North of the line running through the center of the Dome of the Rock in an east-west direction. Moreover, it now seems clear that before .the Golden Gate was constructed, the entrance to the Temple Mount from outside the city, was in exactly the same location. **Recently, part of an archway** was discovered, directly beneath the Golden Gate. This **partial arch definitely belonged to an older gate."**

CUPOLA

A cupola is located inside what was once the Holy of Holies of the Temple." In Arabic, this *"cupola"* is called *Qubbat el-arwah*, or **Dome of the Spirits**. In Sinai, where the glory of the Lord appeared before the whole community of Israel, Moses and Aaron addressed the Lord as "**God Of the Spirits of all mankind**; *Num. 27:16, Ezekiel 37*, and *Job 12:10*. **Dome of the spirits** is certainly an appropriate name to mark the dwelling place of the Lord's Name, the **Center Of His Divine Presence.**

But, this cupola also has another Arabic name; *Qubbat el-alouah*, **Dome of the Tablets**. In the Holy of Holies of Soloman's Temple was kept the Ark of the Covenant, containing the two stone tablets of the law given to Moses on Mount Sinai, according to M. de Vogue. In his book, <u>Le Temple de Jerusalem</u>

(Noblet and Baudry : Paris 1864, page 105), the name **Dome of the Tablets** was given to this cupola because it is dedicated to the memory of the **Tablets of the Law**. Josephus, the eyewitness Jewish Historian, describes in great detail certain features of the Temple.Josephus lived before and after the destruction of the Temple in 70 AD.

BEDROCK

Dr. Asher Kaufman asserts, "The Holy of Holies in the Second Temple preserved the site of the Holy of Holies in the First Temple. The conclusion, therefore, is that the actual **Ark of the Covenant**, which the people of Israel carried through the desert to the promised land, **rested on the exposed bedrock** sheltered by the unassuming cupola known as the Dome of the Tablets! Thus, this **bedrock is surely one of the most authentically preserved remnants of a sacred past** that has survived from the holiest building in Israel's history, the **actual stone on which the Ark of the Covenant rested.**"

Dr. Kaufman has laid out the dimensions of the Temple as was positioned on the Temple Mount, based on his own observations, aerial photographs and literacy evidence.

MOUNT MORIAH

This all corresponds to the stones which were seen by Dr. Zelev Yeivin from a Moslem Excavation project. The wall seen by Dr. Yeivin helps to confirm the location of the Temple, North of the Dome of the Rock. The Temple Mount is called **Mount Moriah,** *2 Chron. 3:1.* A description of Solomon's Temple and its dimensions are presented in *1 Kings 6,* and *2 Chron. 3-4.* King Solomon used the Tabernacle Tent of David as a pattern for the Temple.

The Tabernacle Tent of David was set up first, then the Temple was built later. So it will be again, as in days of old, *Amos 9:11.* The Tabernacle was placed in the Temple of Solomon with the Ark of the Covenant. *1 Kings 8:4-6.* **God chose the Temple Mount, Mount Moriah as the resting place for the Tabernacle and the Temple,** *1 Chron. 21:18 - 22:6* and *2 Chron. 3:1.*

The Dome need not be destroyed for the Jewish Tabernacle to be restored. In the first place, the **Tabernacle was merely a tent.** Yet,the **Tabernacle of David was also a Temple or Holy Place to house the Sacred Vessels.** The same Tabernacle will be found and raised as it were from the dead. *Amos 9:11.* The Jewish people will say, *"blessed is He that cometh in the Name of the Lord and He will* R*eturn," Matthew 23:39.* At first, the house of the vessels will merely be the Tabernacle tent of David, as in the beginning, *Amos 9:11, Ezek. 37:26-28.* **Later, in the millennial, a more elaborate temple, or covering over the mount, will be erected, *Ezek. 40-46.***

In 1979, the highly respected Pictorial Archive, in Jerusalem issued its new maps on the historical geography of the Bible lands; Hebrew University's Shlomo Margalit, served as Jerusalem's consultant, and the maps were printed by the survey of Israel. The map of Jerusalem, during the Second Temple period, shows an **alternative Temple location,** the **location suggested by Dr. Asher Kaufman's research.**

155

The Jerusalem Rabbis today, know where the original Temple sat.

📖 **Revelation 11:1-3,** *"¹And there was given me a reed like unto a rod: and the angel stood, saying, **Rise, and measure the temple of God, and the altar, and them that worship therein**. ²But, the court, which is without the temple, leaves out, and measure it not; for it is given unto the Gentiles: and the holy city shall they tread under foot forty and two months. ³And, I will give power unto my two witnesses, and they shall prophesy a thousand two hundred and threescore days, clothed in sackcloth."*

For three and half years, the moderate Moslem Arabs, and the Jewish people, will peacefully co-exist. **The Jewish Tabernacle on the North side of the Mount and the Moslem Dome of the Rock on the South side, as given to the Moslem-Gentiles**. The Cloud of Glory will rest over the Temple and astonishing things will happen. Does the **Tabernacle** or **Temple** have to be **restored on the original site upon Mount Moriah? Yes.** Why is this so? Because Mount Moriah was the place where Abraham was to offer up his son Isaac, the ancestor of Israel, *Gen. 22:2*.It was decreed by God to King David, that the Temple, and the Tabernacle, be set upon Moriah, at the place of Arnan's threshing floor before the Lord. This was to remain the designated place. It could not be in West Jerusalem, because this was not the land allotted to Judah and the ruling family of David. This is the way it was in days of old.

The terms **"Tabernacle"** and **"Temple"** are used interchangeably in the scriptures. A house to contain the vessels could be a tabernacle **tent** or a more elaborate

building. For example, **Jesus' body** is referred to as a Temple, *St. John 2:19*, and as a Tabernacle *Heb. 9:11*.

"Tabernacle" in Hebrew is *cukkah,* meaning **hut, booth, cottage, covert, pavilion, or tent.** *"Tabernacle"* in Greek is *skene,* **tent, hut, or habitation.** *"Temple"* in Hebrew is *heykal,* **a large public building, house, or habitation.** *"Temple"* in Greek is *maos,* **dwelling, or shrine**. Also, the *hieron* is sometimes used which means **sacred place, or sanctuary, or temple.**

Thus, the Tabernacle will be **erected prior to anti-Christ.** *Dan. 9:27,* and *Matt. 24:15, Amos 9:11,* this is what he will defile, for the Holy Place is synonymous with the Tabernacle, *Ex. 25:8, Ex. 26:33, 28:29, Heb. 9:2*. **The Tabernacle therefore, is the Tribulation Temple.**

COHENITE PRIESTHOOD ESTABLISHED

A school has been established in Jerusalem for the training and preparation of the priesthood in time for the repitching of the Tabernacle and the subsequent Sacrificial Memorial. The priest's garments are being weaved. Even the formula for the ancient dye of blue garment fringes has been rediscovered, *Numbers 15.* This is the beginning of the **Cohenite Priesthood**. The school was **established in 1978 by Rabbi Motti Hachohen in the Moslem quarter of old Jerusalem.**② A more recent article on the Temple Restoration can be found in the October 16, 1989 issue of Time Magazine. This article mentions, among others, Rabbi Schlomo Goren and Zev Golan, of the Temple Institute, in Jerusalem.

WESTERN WALL

The Western Wall around the Temple Mount was never destroyed, even though all the temple buildings were destroyed. Today, Herod's temple lies in ruins 52 feet under the surface west of the Dome of the Rock. Thirty-two known caves and cisterns are under the Temple Mount. The stones were ten feet long and 6 feet wide. One has been found underneath weighing about 445 tons. It was a part of the Temple.

It is believed by the Jewish people that the Divine presence never left the Western Wall. The Western Wall is the only **remnant of the Temple Mount** that has survived. All Jews were told to pray facing the Temple, *1 Kings 8:30-48*. Jews from all over the world come to pray at this wall. This was prophesied by Isaiah. "And I will bring them to my holy mountain and I will make them joyful in my house of prayer. And I will make your sanctuaries desolate." *Lev. 26:31,* is interpreted by Jewish sages as meaning that **they still have sanctity of sanctuaries even when they are desolate.**

📖 **2 Chron. 7:16,** *"For now I have chosen and sanctified this house so that my name shall be there for ever and **my eyes and my heart will be there all the days.**"*

Even when it is destroyed, it remains in its sanctity.

HOLY LIGHT NEVER CEASES

The Jews believe, "The divine presence will never leave the Western Wall, for behold, *He stands behind our wall*," S*ong* of *Solomon 2:9.* Rabbi Jacob Ethlinger wrote, "There is a **holy light on the temple and it does not cease** even when the temple lies in ruins; it will never cease! This holy light has a greater influence there than in any other place, for the site of the temple is opposite the gate of heaven which will never close, and there the holy light always **shines with greater strength and greater brilliance**."

Therefore, Marmonides, the 12th Century Rabbi, wrote, "the divine presence is never abrogated because the holy light which sanctified the temple has never stopped and never will stop." On this it was said; "The divine presence never leaves the Western Wall, that is the concealed holy light." *Ps. 137:7*, The enemies said, "Raze it, Raze it". But they only succeeded as far as the base, but could not touch the base itself.

Ps. 122:3, Jerusalem is built as a city that is compacted together. *"Compact"*, in Hebrew, from *Kawbaw*, **meaning to recouple or rejoin.** In the Six Days War of 1967, East and West Jerusalem were recoupled or rejoined.

Ps. 122:6, In that same generation, "pray for the peace of Jerusalem; they shall prosper that love thee." Verse 7-9, "peace be within thy Walls, and prosperity within thy palaces. For my brethren and companion's sakes I will now say, Peace be within thee." However, as Rabbi Ben Zion Alkalai wrote, the area is endowed with a certain sanctity.

"But as the great Jewish sage, Maimonides, of the 12th Century wrote, "Therefore, it is permissible to offer all the sacrifices, although the Temple no longer exists. Unfortunately, there are certain pre-requisites lacking, and so we cannot bring sacrifices. **For example, we are all afflicted with ritual impurity from touching the dead and we do not have the Ashes of the Red Heifer which are needed to effect purification.**

Behind this wall, children cry to their father in Heaven, *Numbers 19.*

PRAY FOR THE PEACE OF JERUSALEM.

THE FOLLY OF
REPLACEMENT THEOLOGY

Chapter Seventeen

There are those who teach the church that spiritual Israel replaced natural Israel, that the New Jerusalem replaced literal Jerusalem on earth and the New Testament replaced or terminated the Old Testament. This doctrine began with St. Augustine who borrowed it from the scholar Oregin's Spiritualizing the Bible.

In the Fourth Century AD, some even taught that Rome was the eternal city that replaced Jerusalem. There are those who teach that all Old Testament prophecies related to Israel have been fulfilled, that there are no more Old Testament Scriptures to be fulfilled, and that Israel as a Nation is finished, having no relevance to End-time events today.These teachings are usually referred to as "replacement theology."

Let us examine the scriptures to ascertain the validity,or folly, of replacement theology.

The term "*Israel*", or *Israel* in Hebrew, means the **people of God.** Israel was God's chosen people and therefore were not numbered among the nations, *Numbers 23:9.* Israel is God's chosen. We as Christians are the called , called out from among the Gentiles. The word "*Gentile*", in both Hebrew and Greek, **means nations or heathen.** God never disowned Israel or disowned His promises. God's promise to Abraham, Isaac, Jacob, Moses, and David ,concerning the promised land, as Israel's inheritance was an unconditional promise.

📖 **Ezek. 36:22,** *"Therefore say unto the House of Israel, Thus saith the Lord God; I do not this for your sakes, O*

161

House of Israel, but for mine Holy Name's sake, which ye have profaned among the heathen, whither ye went."

📖 **Ps. 89:28-37,** ²⁸"*My mercy will I keep for him for evermore, and **My covenant shall stand** fast with him. ²⁹His seed also will I make to endure for ever, and his throne as the days of heaven. ³⁰If his children forsake My law, and walk not in My judgments; ³¹if they break My statutes, and keep not My commandments; ³²then will I visit their transgression with the rod, and their iniquity with stripes. ³³Nevertheless, My loving-kindness will I not utterly take from him, **nor suffer my faithfulness to fail.** ³⁴My covenant will I not break, nor alter the thing that is gone out of My lips. ³⁵Once have I sworn by My holiness that I will not lie unto David. ³⁶His seed shall endure for ever, and his throne as the sun before Me. ³⁷**It shall be established forever** as the moon, and as a faithful witness in heaven. Selah.*"

HEBREW

Our Bible came from the Hebrews of Israel. The Hebrews originated the concept of "**One God**." This concept is contrasted with "polytheism", or a plurality of Gods. Islam was a late-comer. Therefore, our Bible is an original, unique Bible. **Jesus Christ was of the Hebrew Nation.** God the Father could have selected another nation for Jesus to have been born in, but He chose Israel's family and the **lineage of King David.** Jesus spoke in the Hebrew language. The Hebrew language was still existent and vital in the days of the Apostle Paul. *Acts 21:40, "And when he had given him license, Paul stood on the stairs, and beckoned with the hand unto the people. And when there was made a great silence, **he spake unto them in the Hebrew tongue**, saying," Acts 22:2,"And when they heard that he spake in the Hebrew tongue to them, they kept the*

162

more silence: and he saith," Acts 26:14, **"And when we were all fallen to the earth, I heard a voice speaking unto me,saying in the Hebrew tongue, Saul, Saul, why persecutest thou me? It is hard for thee to kick against the pricks."**

In the <u>Bible</u>, religious **Israel was likened** to the **Olive Tree**; redeemed Israel, the **Vine;** national Israel, the **Fig Tree**; and apostate Israel, the **Bramble Bush,** *Joel 1, Jer. 11:16, Jer. 24:5, Judges 9:8-15.*

WHERE REPLACEMENT THEOLOGY BEGAN

Replacement theology was not taught in the early Christian church. **It began in earnest with Constantine, the Roman Emperor, at the Council of Nicea, 325 AD.** The theology was perpetuated during the Dark Ages and adopted by many to this day. What does God say about Israel and the continuity of Israel as a nation?

EQUALITY IN CHRIST JESUS

At this point in the book, I want to challenge anyone who can point to one single scripture to substantiate replacement theology. Where is the scripture that says the Church replaced Israel? You may produce *Gal. 3:27-29, 27"For as many of you as have been baptized into Christ have put on Christ. 28There is neither Jew nor Greek, there is neither bond nor free, there is neither male nor female: for ye are all one in Christ Jesus. 29And if ye be Christ's, then are ye Abraham's seed, and heirs according to the promise."* But notice, **this scripture does not say there is no more Jew, no more relevance to Israel.** Rather, the statement merely **portrays the equality of Jew and Gentile in Christ Jesus,** or in God's plan of Salvation. In *Rom. 3:22,* the context is sin and not a premise for replacing Jew with

Gentile. *Rom. 3:22, "Even the righteousness of God which is by faith of Jesus Christ unto all and upon all them that believe: for there is no difference:"*

Rom. 10:12-13, reinforces the concept, that the God of Israel is also the God of the Gentiles or Christians. *Gal. 3:28,* is emphasizing that now both Jew and Gentile have access to one God.*Gal. 3:28, "There is neither Jew nor Greek, there is neither bond nor free, there is neither male nor female: for ye are all one in Christ Jesus."* **We Gentiles,** through Jesus Christ, are **now partakers and fellow heirs with Israel.**

📖 **Eph. 2:12,14,** [12]*"That at that time ye were without Christ, being aliens from the commonwealth of Israel, and strangers from the covenants of promise, having no hope, and without God in the world:* [14]*For* **He** *is our peace, who hath* **made both one,** *and hath broken down the middle wall of partition between us;"*

Let us repeat there is no scripture to support the replacement theology, or that Christians have superseded, or replaced Israel, is not in the <u>Bible.</u> Israel was the offspring of Abraham, Isaac, and Jacob. These patriarchs are the roots of Israel, the good Olive Tree, *Rom. 11. "For the Lord's portion is His people; Jacob is the lot of his inheritance," Deut.32:9.*

📖 **Ps.105:6-11.**The Psalmist David said, [6]*"oh ye seed of Abraham, his servant, ye children of Jacob, his chosen.* [7]*He is the Lord our God; His judgments are in all the earth.* [8]*He hath remembered His covenant forever, the word which He commanded to a thousand generations.* [9]*Which covenant He made with Abraham, and His oath unto Isaac,* [10]*And confirmed the same unto Jacob for a law, and to Israel for an everlasting covenant,*

164

11Saying, unto thee will I give the Land of Canaan, the lot of your inheritance."

Even if there were only ten years to a generation here, the Covenant and the Nation of Israel would still exist for ten thousand years. It has only been four thousand years since Abraham.

📖 **Jer. 31:35-37,**35*"Thus saith the Lord, which giveth the sun for a light by day, and the ordinances of the moon and of the stars for a light by night, which divideth the sea when the waves thereof roar; **the Lord of Hosts is His Name:**36If those ordinances depart from before Me, saith the Lord, then the seed of Israel also shall cease from being a nation before Me for ever. 37Thus saith the Lord; if heaven above can be measured, and the foundations of the earth searched out beneath, I will also cast off all the Seed of Israel for all that they have done, saith the Lord."*

As this book goes to print, the sun, moon, and stars are still shining. The heaven has not been measured. Therefore, Israel is still a nation before the Lord and still relevant to God's Word and the fulfillment of Bible Prophecy. Even though the Jerusalem rulers brought wrath upon Israel in 70 AD, and it was left desolate**, Jesus promised the restoration of Israel and Jerusalem.** *Matt. 23:36,38,* 36*"Verily I say unto you, All these things shall come upon this generation.* 38*Behold, your house is left unto you desolate." Luke 21:24.*

These prophecies are referring directly to literal Jerusalem. *Matt. 21:10-11.* **Jesus** went into the Temple. This was the **Natural Temple** he went into, because he was the **Spiritual Temple** already. *Matt. 21:12, St. John 2:21,*

Matt. 23:37, Matt. 24:1,3, Luke 21:20-24, Luke 24:41,52, Acts 1:12, Acts 3:1.

As Paul stated, God did not cast away His people Israel, but only some of the branches were broken off, because of unbelief, *Rom. 11:16-24.* The tree is still alive, and we Gentiles were grafted into that tree through Jesus Christ. If a branch is grafted into a tree, and the tree dies,or is cut down,what happens to the branch? If Israel as a whole is cut down, would that not also destroy us Gentile Christians who were grafted in?

COMING OF JESUS IN TWO PARTS

Rather, Israel is blind in part. **That is, the Coming of Jesus is in two parts.** He came to earth two thousand years ago through the virgin birth. **He came then to suffer and die for mankind.**

📖 **Heb. 12:12-13,** [12]*"Wherefore lift up the hands which hang down, and the feeble knees; [13]And make straight paths for your feet, lest that which is lame be turned out of the way; but let it rather be healed."*

He is coming back in glory to deliver Israel from its enemies, and to reign in glory, fulfilling all of the Messianic Promises.

📖 **Rom. 11:26,** *"And so all Israel shall be saved: as it is written, There **shall come out of Zion the Deliverer**, and shall turn away ungodliness from Jacob:"*

📖 **Zech. 14:3-4,** [3]*"Then shall the Lord go forth, and fight against those nations, as when he fought in the day of battle. [4]And **his feet shall stand in that day upon the Mount of Olives,** which is before Jerusalem* *on the east, and the Mount of Olives shall cleave in the midst thereof toward the east and toward the west, and there shall be a very great valley; and half of the mountain shall remove toward the north, and half of it toward the south ."*

When Israel reads of the Second Coming of Messiah in the Old Testament, they understand, **but cannot yet see His First Coming to earth.** Therefore, **blindness in part** has happened to Israel, **until the Fullness of the Gentiles** come in, *Roman 11:1, 16-21, 24-26.* **The Deliverer is the Messiah, the Christ.** There is a 2,000 year gap between.

📖 **Zech. 9:9-10,** ⁹*"Rejoice greatly, O daughter of Zion; shout, O daughter of Jerusalem: behold, thy King cometh unto thee: he is just, and having salvation; lowly, and riding upon an ass, and upon a colt, the foal of an ass. ¹⁰And I will cut off the chariot from Ephraim, and the horse from Jerusalem, and the battle bow shall be cut off: and he shall speak peace unto the heathen: and his dominion shall be from sea even to sea, and from the river even to the ends of the earth."*

Jesus came into Jerusalem riding the donkey, but did not fulfill *verse 10*, for Jerusalem was destroyed in 70 AD. One may ask how can we identify the Jewish people? How do we know those people in Israel are Israel? First of all, persecutors do not seem to have any problem identifying these people. Haman knew who they were. So did the Spanish, the Crusaders, Titus, and Adolf Hitler. Israel has preserved their culture, their language.They are identifiable no matter where they go.

THE TRUE JEWS

The **Apostle Paul equates Israel as the True Jews and gave eight marks of identification.** The **Adoption**, the **Shekinah Glory,** the **Covenants**, the **Law**, the **Temple Service,** the **Promises** concerning the land of Israel, the **Fathers,** and the **Messiah from their nation.**

📖 **Rom. 9:4,** *"Who are Israelites; to whom pertaineth the adoption, and the glory, and the covenants, and the giving of the law, and the service of God, and the promises;"*

The land which Israel possesses today is the same as their original ancient land. The Return was promised, it has been accomplished. It has been phenomenal, miraculous. **It has not been fulfilled by God because of their righteousness, but because of Gods promise to their fathers and to reestablish the Name of the Lord in Israel and Jerusalem,***Ezek. 36:22,23,32.* **The re-gathering of Israel was also promised unconditionally in the Moabic Covenant,** the second covenant God gave to Moses.

📖 *Deut. 29:1, "These are the words of the covenant, which the Lord commanded Moses to make with the children of Israel in the land of Moab,beside the covenant which he made with them in Horeb."*

This **identity of Israel will be reinforced and confirmed** before the world, with the restoration of the Tabernacle, Ashes of the Red Heifer, and the Shekinah over the Temple Mount. *Amos 9:11, Lev. 9:23* Israel is unique in that the **Jewish identity,** or inheritance is **traced through the mother.** One who has a Jewish mother is heir, *Gen. 3:15, Gal. 4:4.* Timothy had a Jewish mother and therefore observed the ritual of circumcision, *Acts 16:1-3.*The boundaries of the land of Israel were promised to Isaac,

168

Jacob, and his twelve sons. However, Abraham had other seed outside the lineage of Isaac and Jacob; *ie,* through Ishmael, and six sons by Keturah. *Gen. 25:1, "Then again Abraham took a wife, and her name was Keturah."*

Jacob was both **blessed** and made **crippled,** *Gen.32:24-32.* The **people of Israel have been both blessed and crippled throughout their history.** Both prosperous, and persecuted, scattered and re-gathered, blind and with sight, honored and dishonored.**They have not been consumed, but have survived** the vicissitudes of time, **as a witness to all nations of God's Timeless Promise to the Sons of Jacob,** *Mal. 3:6.*

ARK OF THE COVENANT

Chapter Eighteen

📖 **Exodus 25:10-22,** *¹⁰"and they shall make an **ark** of shittim wood: two cubits and a half shall be the length thereof, and a cubit and a half the breadth thereof, and a cubit and a half the height thereof. ¹¹And **thou shalt overlay it with pure gold,** within and without shalt thou overlay it, and shalt make upon it **a crown of gold** round about. ¹²And thou shalt cast **four rings of gold** for it, and put them in the four corners thereof; and two rings shall be in the one side of it, and two rings in the other side of it. ¹³And thou shalt make staves of shittim wood, and **overlay them with gold.** ¹⁴And thou shalt put the staves into the rings by the sides of the ark, that the ark may be borne with them. ¹⁵The **staves** shall be in the rings of the ark: they shall not be taken from it. ¹⁶**And thou shalt put into the ark the testimony which I shall give thee.** ¹⁷And thou shalt make a **mercy seat of pure gold**: two cubits and a half shall be the length thereof, and a cubit and a half the breadth thereof. ¹⁸And thou shalt make **two cherubim of gold**, of beaten work shalt thou make them, in the two ends of the mercy seat. ¹⁹And make one cherub on the one end, and the other cherub on the other end: even of the mercy seat shall ye make the cherubim on the two ends thereof. ²⁰And the cherubim shall stretch forth their wings on high, covering the mercy seat with their wings, and their faces shall look one to another; toward the mercy seat shall the faces of the cherubim be. ²¹And thou shalt put the **mercy seat** above upon the ark; and in the ark thou shalt put the testimony that I shall give thee. ²²And there I will meet with thee, and **I will commune with thee from above the mercy seat**, from **between the two cherubim,** which are upon the ark of* *the testimony, of all things which I will give thee in commandment unto the children of Israel"*

📖 **Hebrew 9:3-5,** 3*"And after the second veil, the tabernacle, with is called the Holiest of all; 4Which had the golden censer, and the **ark of the covenant** overlaid round about with gold, wherein was the **golden pot that had manna,** and **Aaron's rod** that budded, and the **tables of the covenant;** 5And over it the cherubims of glory shadowing the mercy seat; of which we cannot now speak particularly."*

THE ARK HIDDEN

It is written into the Hebrew <u>Midrash</u> that Solomon built subterranean tunnels under Old Jerusalem to hide the Ark of the Covenant and the Tabernacle.

It is written in <u>2 Maccabees</u> Chapter 2, that **Jeremiah hid the Ark of the Covenant, the Tabernacle and the Golden Altar** of Incense. This document, written about 200 BC., states that prior to the Babylonian siege of Jerusalem, Jeremiah and his group took these articles to Mount Nebo and looked over into the heritage of Israel, where Moses looked, and then went thither and hid them in a hallow cave. Perhaps temporarily, in the caves at Qumran, due West of Mount Nebo, in the land of inheritance (Israel). The <u>Maccabees</u> further states that Jeremiah prophesied that when Israel would be re-gathered into their land from the Babylonian captivity, **the Ark and Tabernacle would be found and returned.** This would answer the questions to why the Essenes were gathered at Qumran in the first place. This was an important depository of the Hebrew scriptures from which they copied the <u>Dead Sea Scrolls</u>. A monastery going back to at least the 9th or 10th Century BC The Holy Ark was still in Jerusalem during the reign of King Josiah,*2 Chron. 35:1-3*. Babylon besieged Jerusalem in *2 Chron.36*. The Golden Altar of Incense was in the Second Temple at Jerusalem, *Luke 1*. The Ark of the Covenant was probably not in the Second Temple, but was hidden underground nearby.There are several Rabbis in Jerusalem who believe the Ark is underground in Old Jerusalem, including Rabbi Zvi.

There is a certain underground tunnel there,sealed up at this time, 1992. This would all harmonize with the <u>Midrash</u>, the <u>Maccabees</u>, and other evidence we have discovered at Qumran. It would also corroborate with,

📖 **Hos. 3:4-5,** *4"For the children of Israel shall abide many days without a king, and without a prince, and without a sacrifice, and without an image, and without an ephod, and without teraphim: 5Afterward shall the children of Israel return, and seek the Lord their God, and David their King; and shall fear the Lord and His goodness in the latter days."*

📖 **Amos 9:11,** *"In that day will I raise up the Tabernacle of David that is fallen, and close up the breaches thereof; and I will raise up his ruins, and I will build it as in the days of old:"*

NOT IN BABYLON

Even if Babylon took the Ark, the scriptures testify that they returned all the vessels which they took.

📖 **Ezra 5:14-15,** 14*"And the **vessels** also of gold and silver **of the House of God**, which **Nebuchadnezzar took out** of the Temple that was in Jerusalem, and brought them into the temple of Babylon, those did Cyrus, the King, take out of the temple of Babylon, and they were delivered unto one, whose name was*

Sheshbazzar, whom he had made governor; [15]*And said unto him,* **Take these vessels,** *go, carry them* **into the Temple** *that is in Jerusalem, and let the house of God be builded in his place."*

MOSES' ARK
NOT IN EGYPT, NOT IN HEAVEN

The Ark is not in Egypt because it was still in Jerusalem long after some say it was taken to Egypt, *2 Chron. 35.* The Ark of the Covenant which Moses made **is not in Heaven** as some say, using *Rev. 11:19,* "And the Temple of God was opened in Heaven, and there was seen in His Temple the Ark of his Testament: and there were lightning's, and voices, and thundering, and an earthquake, and great hail." **John saw the true Ark in the true Tabernacle, in the reality of Heaven.** The same Ark or pattern from which Moses made the model. **John saw the same thing Moses saw in Heaven.**

📖 **Ex. 25:40,** *"And look that thou make them after their pattern, which was showed thee in the mount."*

Moses merely made an earthly model from the pattern of the Heavenly reality.

📖 **Heb. 8:2,5,** [2]*A minister of the sanctuary, and of the true Tabernacle, which* **the Lord pitched,** *and not man.* [5]*Who serve unto the example and shadow of heavenly things, as Moses was admonished of God when he was about to make the Tabernacle: for,* **See, saith he, that thou make all things according to the pattern showed to thee in the mount."*

Therefore the real, true, original Ark never left Heaven.

173

DISCOVERY

Dr. David A. Lewis of Springfield MO., relates an episode in his book "Prophecy 2000," which again corresponds to the Jewish Midrash, the Maccabees and other evidence presented in this book. This episode involves Rabbi Motti Hacohen, founder of the School in 1978, for the training and preparation of the Cohenite Jewish Temple Priesthood. Dr. Lewis explains that the first time he and Mrs. Lewis met Rabbi Hacohen was on a cold, rainy February day. After Rabbi Hacohen had assembled a small model of the temple and explained his vision for the school and for the rebuilding of the temple, he began to talk to us about some of the excavations under the Temple Mountain. He told how he was working late at night with Rabbi Getz, and a group of archeologists and rabbinical scholars. Hacohen told of how they were excavating the lower level of the Western Wall of the Temple Mountain. At one point during the night, they came to a doorway in the Western Wall. Passing through this doorway, the crew entered a fairly long tunnel. At the end of the tunnel, Rabbi Hacohen said, "**I saw the golden Ark** that once stood in the Holy Place of **the Temple of the Almighty.**" It was covered over with old, dried animal skins of some kind. (**The Tabernacle was made of animal skins** , *Ex. 25.)* However **one gold, gleaming end of the Ark was visible.** He could see the loops or rounds of gold through which the poles of Acacia wood could be thrust so that the Ark could be properly carried by four dedicated Levites. Hacohen and his friends rushed out to the home of Chief Rabbi Shlomo Goren. They awakened the Rabbi and excitedly told him that they had discovered the Ark of the Covenant! Rabbi Goren said, "We are ready for this event. We have already prepared the poles of Acacia wood and have Levites who can be standing by in the morning to carry out the Ark in triumph." At the earliest dawning of the day, Hacohen, Goren, and the others went to the tunnel. To their shocked amazement they found that during the night, the **Moslems had erected a wooden form and poured a concrete wall sealing off the tunnel that would give access to the Ark of the Covenant.** Dr. David Lewis asked, "why didn't you break through the concrete. It would have been easy to do". I begged Rabbi Goren to give us permission to break through the wall, but Rabbi Goren replied, "every time we do anything around the Temple Mount, it creates problems for Israel with the Arabs, the United Nations, and the United States.

It seems to make everybody upset, so we will not break through. We know where the Holy Object is and **when we receive the word from the Almighty, we will go in and recover it.** Don't worry, the **Moslems** revere the Ark as much as we do, and **they would be afraid to touch it.**"

Certainly, the finding and recovery of the **Ashes of the Red Heifer** would be to the Jewish people and these Rabbis, **the word from the Almighty.** The Moslem recognition of the Ashes of the Red Cow would also allow Israel to recover the Ark. Another project in search for the Ark of the Covenant involves the Ron Wyatt Team in the Jerusalem area. Ron has already been involved in other discoveries, including Noah's Ark in Turkey, and Pharaoh's Chariot Wheels, in the Red Sea.

All things are now coming together in preparation for the Grand and Golden completion of the Hebrew Renaissance. The release of the Jews from the Soviet Union and the search for the Ashes and the Temple Treasures.During my experience and involvement with archeological expeditions in Israel, I have been in contact with many interesting people. I have been enthusiastically involved in several archeological finds. I do this for Israel, for validation of the Holy scriptures, and in the interest of Bible Prophecy Fulfillment. I enjoy being a part of all this.From the very beginning, and all through the 1980's and into the 1990's, I have maintained that the ancient Mosaic Ark of the Covenant was hidden beneath the Temple Mount in the Old City of Jerusalem. According to the Second Maccabees, Jeremiah prophesied the Ark would be returned from a temporary hiding place to Jerusalem. Solomon built a subterranean chamber especially for hiding the Ark, according to the Jewish Midrash.

THE ARK IS NOT IN ETHIOPIA BUT UNDER JERUSALEM

I have received many reports from Israel concerning certain Rabbis and Archeologists, who a few years ago, actually saw the Ark beneath the city of Jerusalem. The CBS television network aired a special nationwide program on Friday night, May 15, 1992, presenting evidence to validate the accuracy of the Bible. During this program, Rabbi Getz of Jerusalem was interviewed. He announced that he was one of those who saw the Ark of the Covenant in a tunnel beneath the city in 1981. Rabbi Schlomo Goren, the former Chief Rabbi of Israel, also confirmed this. Let it be noted they themselves chose to make the announcement to the world. Therefore, the true original Ark is not in Ethiopia as some have supposed from an ancient legend. We have been saying all along the **Ark of the Covenant is under Jerusalem.**

**EVERYTHING IS IN PLACE
AND COMING TOGETHER
FOR THE JOYOUS AND TRIUMPHANT COMING
OF MESSIAH!**

A DOOR OF HOPE,
IN THE VALLEY OF ACHOR

Chapter Nineteen

After studying and researching into the Biblically supported Hebrew Renaissance, of *Amos 9:11*, I became involved with various archeological search teams in the early 1980's. There had been several people searching for the Ashes of the Red Heifer sacrifice, and the vessels of the Jewish Temple.

The Essenes, the Sons of Zadok, and the Zealots hid the Temple Treasures and Scrolls in the caves of the Qumran area, as we explained in Chapter 11, Ashes of Adventure. They even booby trapped some of the caves to prevent the Romans from finding the treasure. They used devices such as catapult stones and various stone trigger mechanisms. There have been cave-ins and falling rocks during our digs, but fortunately only minor injuries have resulted.

THE DIG

In 1986, I spent a month in Israel with a team in the Judean Desert. We stayed on the West Jordan Bank and I felt safer in Israel than in major cities of the United States. As we were digging in the red dolomite rock caves of the Judean Desert, one could not help but look at the red, dusty, charred walls and think of John the Baptist, the Essenes, the Sons of Zadok, the Zealots and perhaps even Jesus himself, having once walked before these same walls, seeing the same scenery, and dwelling in the same desert.

Here we could look at Mount Nebo, just across the Dead Sea, where Moses viewed the Promised Land. Here we worked feverishly in a cave, wearing a filtered mask as protection from the red dust which is thick in the cave. A sickness, known as dung lung, is a hazard from the red dust

177

of the bat-filled caves. As diggers slashed through the dust, rock and dirt, picks broke up the small rocks, buckets of dirt and rock were passed out of the cave by a bucket brigade, we cheerfully sang, "Rock of Ages," and "This is the Day the Lord has made."

All these sounds of excitement with prophetic anticipation echoed out of the cave into the warm desert air. At times we prayed, as we turned our faces toward Jerusalem. One could not help, but feel a special destiny, thinking that sometime soon a band of searchers would behold with their own eyes the greatest archeological discoveries in history, the Jewish Tabernacle Treasures. When the Jewish Remnant hid the Ashes of the Red Heifer in 70 AD, they placed the ashes in a bronze-copper container called the *"pitcher"*, or *Kalil*. They hid it in a cave, and under it a scroll giving an inventory and explanation of all things mentioned in the Copper Scroll. All the Temple Treasures, *Acts 3:20-21*. They disclosed this information on one of the Dead Sea Scrolls. The Essenes are they who also copied the Dead Sea Scrolls from the manuscripts of the scriptures. The Treasure Scroll, known as the Copper Scroll, was found in 1952, in the Judean Desert. Let us read some excerpts from the Copper Scroll.

"In the pit, which is in the KLHM, in it's North tithe vessels and garments: Its entrance is under the Western Corner. In the tomb which is in the Waddy Ha Kippa in the Eastern road to Secucah, buried at seven cubits, 32 talents. In the pit adjoining on the North in a hole opening northwards and buried at its mouth: a copy of this document, with an explanation and their measurements and an inventory of each thing and other things. In the inner chamber of the platform of the double gate, facing east, in the Northern entrance, buried at three cubits, hidden there is a pitcher (*Kalil*) in it, one Scroll, under it, 42 talents;" and on and on it goes.In 1988, we returned to the Judean Desert, spending two months, living in a tent, on the desert. We set up a tent next to an Israeli Kubbutz, serving also as a military outpost.During the daytime, we worked in the same place as 1986. The days were long and hard. The rains poured every day the first three weeks we were there. The first month, David Fasold worked with our team. David was a member of a team which reported rediscovering Noah's Ark in the Ararat Mountains of Turkey, in 1985.

Here we were in the desert, spotted with flowers, and fruits beginning to blossom. This was a real-life adventure. The real thing, not just a movie. A situation in which strangers from a far country were pitted against the heat and dust of the desert, scorpions, falling rocks, and cave-ins, in search of the exclusive treasure of the ancient Jewish Temple. All of this is set artistically in the resurrecting desert, under a Mid-Eastern sky, at night glistening with the countless stars. One can look up overhead and see the contour of the constellation, known to the Greeks as Leo the Lion, but known to us as the Lion of the Tribe of Judah. One such night, with the echo of Israeli songs and Mid-Eastern music in the camp, an alarm sounded, and a flare shot into the sky. Within minutes, our team and tent were surrounded by Israeli soldiers, equipped with machine guns for our protection. We later were told a terrorist was thought to be spotted crossing from Jordan into Israel. This reminded us there was still turmoil in the region.

On this dig, we found various artifacts, such as pottery, three to four thousand years old, and a Roman Lamp dated 132 AD., now possessed by Hebrew University.

During the Vendyl Jones archeology expedition, of which I was a part in April, 1988, Joseph Patrick and Benny Arubas of Hebrew University asked for volunteers from our team to

179

participate in a survey of caves in the Judean Desert. As part of a project directed by the Archeology Department of Hebrew University, I agreed to work with that team in surveying caves just North of Qumran.

FLASK OF OIL

We were excavating a cave 2.8 kilometers to the North of Qumran, and about 150 meters to the West of the track which runs between Kibbutz Qalia and Kibbutz Almog, when under the direction of Benny Arubas **a juglet was uncovered containing anointing oil**. **The flask of oil** was found in Cave 14 slightly more than three feet below the surface. It was **hidden between the rocks**, and **wrapped in a covering of palm fibbers**, all intended to protect and preserve the vessel from damage. This probably indicates that the vessel's contents were valuable, and considered worth the trouble of hiding, taking special measures to protect it. The vessel is a globular juglet with a flat base and a cup-rim. It is 10 centimeters high, and its maximal diameter is 7.3 centimeters.

When found, the **vessel was almost completely full up** to the level of the round hole. A small amount of oil, which had spilled out through this hole in the past, had hardened, and was stuck to the vessel's side.

Preliminary analysis was undertaken by Dr. Elka Trito, of the Pharmaceutical School of Hodassah University Hospital, Jerusalem and Dr. G. Schiller of the Vulcani Institute. In the light of evidence from ancient sources and from the fact that no modern plant oil definitely resembles that which was found in the juglet, the possibility should be considered that **this oil was extracted from a now extinct plant**. The oil seems to be composed of balsam oil, or (*apabalsamum*) and other oils, and compounds. It is a perfume oil. **The balsam**

plant has been extinct for 1,500 years. From all indications this is the *Shemen Afarshiman,* or **Holy Anointing Oil** used to anoint the Tabernacle Vessels, Priests and Kings of Israel. It was still in existence in the Second Temple period. *Ex. 30, and the oil was used over 2000 years ago to anoint also the vessels of the Temple or Tabernacle.*

According to the Jewish Rabbinical <u>Midrash</u>, the flask of oil was hidden before Jerusalem was destroyed in 70 AD. and was prophesied to be restored in Mashiach's time.

Mashiach is the Hebrew Word for *"Messiah"*. **The flask of oil was found in April, 1988 during Israel's 40th Anniversary as a modern nation-state**. It was listed in the <u>Copper Scroll</u>.

Therefore, giving credibility to the scroll, and adding evidence that the other 60 items of the Temple are hidden in the area, and will be found. **Even the Stones, the Oil, and the Temple Treasures are crying out that we are living in Messiah's Time, the Generation of His coming, in Glory.** It was essential this oil be found for the prophetic fulfillment related to the restoration of the Tabernacle, as stated in the scriptures.

THE DOOR OF HOPE

In the Judean Desert, there is a Door Of Hope,

📖 **Hos. 2:15**, *"And I will give her, her vineyards from thence, and* ***the Valley of Achor for a Door Of Hope****: and she shall sing there, as in the days of her youth, and as in the day when she came up out of the land of Egypt."*

Today we see the vineyard, in this valley, a beautiful fertile grape vineyard, as Hosea predicted would be, when Israel returned to their land from the nations. So where is the Door Of Hope? There is an entrance to Hope somewhere in this valley. The **Hope of Israel and the world is the Messiah, Jesus Christ, Yeshua,** but there is a door specifically in Achor that will lead to the Restoration of the Tabernacle, Zion, and ultimately the Return of the King in Glory, *Ps. 102:13-18*.

The Door is an entrance to a cave, wherein lies buried the hidden **Ashes of the Red Cow**, and **other Vessels** required to open up a road leading to the Return of the King of Kings. Then they shall say, *"Blessed is He that cometh in the Name of the Lord,"* Matt. 23:39.

RAIDERS OF THE QUMRAN CAVES

Chapter Twenty

I have had the privilege of digging in several caves, with various teams. Several of us had come to believe the treasure was not in any of these caves. We had excavated to bedrock in different caves, and we found no sign of the treasure we were searching for. We believed the major treasures were hidden in another area, perhaps the Qumran area. Toward the close of our 1988 dig, my team friend Gary Collett, his son Andrew, and I began an intensive survey of the Judean Desert in search for a more favorable site.

The Copper Scroll states, "The cave of the *Kalil* is located on the Eastern road from Jericho to Succacah, by the Waddy Ha Kippa." Succacah was one of the six cities of refuge in the Judean wilderness at what is now called Ein Feshca, *Joshua 15:63*. **The Copper Scroll says the cave would have two entrances facing East, and an opening, or hole, in the top.①**

As we examined another area, we concluded **this was it.** This is where the Scroll revealed it was all along. I was amazed. It stood out so dramatically. **Two entrances facing East, an opening in the roof of the cave.** The cave had everything described in the Copper Scroll and more. We crawled almost straight up, clinging to rocks, sprigs, or whatever, to get up into the cave area.

THE WADDY HA KIPPA

There was a very large *waddy* on the south side of the cave. A *"waddy"* is a **dry river bed or canyon.** The Waddy Ha Kippa and Qumran are the same. *Kippa* in Hebrew means **covering, archway, or bridge over.** A *Kippa* is the little cap Orthodox Jews wear as a **covering on their heads.**

The word *Qumran* in Arabic means **crescent moon, covering, archway or bridge over.**
In comparing the Hebrew with Arabic, **Kippa means Qumran.** This is confirmed by a research study regarding the <u>Dead Sea Scrolls</u> of Milliar Burrows, published by Viking Press, New York, 1955.

When looking at the front cave at Qumran, one entrance now faces due East, and the other has been broken off. If filled in as it was originally, it would also face due East, **completing a double entrance facing due East.** At the head of the Qumran Waddy or canyon is a huge **arched covering thus forming a Kippa.** And at the front end of the Waddy is another lower crescent. Thus the Waddy or Valley of the Crescent Moons, as stated in the movie, "The Last Crusade." This was identical to the description of the <u>Copper Scroll.</u>

In 1988, Gary, myself, and several others formed an archeology team. We applied for a permit from the Israeli Government to excavate the caves of Qumran and the permit was granted, another **miracle of God.** In reading the <u>Copper Scroll</u> during the Spring of 1988, I had noticed that in one of the **61 treasure items specified,** the writers would write of the Temple, and the next item, they would write of the Qumran area. What could this mean?

FOUR CAVES

During a survey in the spring of 1989, Gary Collett discovered evidence of the Qumran area being structured by the Essenes and/or Zealots into a **model of the Temple Mount area in Old Jerusalem.** In **all, four caves** form a perfect square between them with Old Testament temple measurements. The West and East caves on the South end answer to the First and Second Temples. The ravine to the

East would be the Valley of Kidron and the hill to the East of the caves and ravine would be the Mount of Olives.

If this is true, there should be **another cave** on the Western slope of the hill, or peak, in line with Cave 4B, **facing East, just as the Red Heifer Cave on the Western slope of the Mount of Olives in Jerusalem is in line with the Eastern Gate.** We looked and the cave is there!

We excavated the caves and found nothing. But wait! The Copper Scroll gives other information in riddle form as to the location of various places which we cannot now disclose. (In the 42 years since their recovery, twenty five per cent of the Dead Sea Scrolls have not been released to the public.) We have now **used photographic frequency analysis** on this area, and other areas, at a certain location, through the facilities of a US. West Coast laboratory. Using this technique, **an underground object was viewed and analytically described as animal ashes in a copper type pot.** We also had a reading on an underground void, or **room** with what appears to be pottery **containing scrolls.** Other treasures have also been indicated. The only way to know for sure is to dig. Items which could be found include: **The *Kalil*, Copper Scroll and other scrolls, the Ephod, *Ex. 28*, Elijah's Mantle, the Essenes Library, and other things.** We have also used a metal detector with our tests at Qumran. I will not reveal in this book the exact location of any of these objects other than to say they are in the general Qumran area.

MY RETURN TO THE VALLEY

Beginning on October 28, 1989, I returned to the Valley of Achor for a month to continue research on the archeology project. I met with various tour groups at Qumran and had the privilege of sharing with them the project at Qumran. The groups included American ministers Reverend Michael Coleman and Dr. David A. Lewis.

185

During this stay in Israel, I stayed at a Kibbutz where there is a dairy operation, a date grove, and a water slide parkway, all in the Judean Desert of the Valley of Achor.They have dairy cows there giving twenty gallons of milk per day. One cow gave 30 gallons a day, setting a new world record. On my first day there, I was invited by Mr. Omer, the Kibbutz Director, to have dinner with him and his family. During dinner, a conversation developed concerning what we were doing in Israel. In response to an inquiry from a young man from England, Mr. Omer replied, "These are the true Zionists." I appreciate this compliment because **we do consider ourselves, proudly, as Biblical Zionists indeed.**

Aubrey Richardson, another team member who lives in Israel, came up with a very interesting thought. When the Essenes,or scribes, were copying the scriptures, if they made one little error such as making a crooked letter, the scroll was no good and was rejected. Yet they could not destroy it. They had to hide or bury it.

SEEKING THE HIDDEN CHAMBER

The <u>Dead Sea Scrolls</u> have these minor errors and are therefore considered rejects. If you were hiding your scrolls, where would you store the good ones and get rid of the rejects. You would more likely bury, or hide the good ones, better, deeper,and more out of sight. The rejects you might place up higher, on top. This is where the reject scrolls were found, on top in the caves of Qumran, indicating that the good scrolls, and perhaps the **complete Essene library is still buried underground.** We believe this will be proven when more scrolls are found and recent scrolls released. We also believe that **Jesus was linked closely to the Essenes, as was John the Baptist.** More will be revealed as to the identity, relationship, and work of

Jesus Christ. As Aubrey pointed out, Jesus came all the way from Nazareth to the Jordan River, in the Valley of Achor, to be baptized by John. Why did he come so far? Why had he come to this particular area? **John the Baptist is the link.**

During my November, 1989 mission in Israel, Gary Collett and myself had a visit and conference with Zev Golan, Director of the Temple Institute in Jerusalem.

We discussed documentation for the validity of the Qumran site. Mr. Golan confirmed that the word *Qumran* means **Kippa,** and thus he established our most profound evidence that we have discovered the location of the Kalil, Scrolls, and other hidden Temple Treasures. In further discussion with Zev,as to how to proceed with our project, we discussed the validity of the photographic frequency modulation tests, to detect underground objects, voids, materials, etc. Our team has been given Exclusive rights by the Israeli Government to explore the Qumran area. Near the area in the desert, we have pinpointed four or five spots where we believe Temple Treasure is hidden including the Ashes of the Red Heifer. We will not reveal these places at this time. We have an exclusive permit by the Israeli Government to do further High Tech tests at these places. This is all we can write or say publicly at this time.

THE ARK AND THE ALTAR

In early 1988, while on the dig with David Fasold, a rediscoverer of Noah's Ark, I informed Mr. Fasold that I believed the Ark of the Covenant and the Altar of Incense had been returned to Jerusalem after the Babylonian captivity. His immediate response was to agree. This was established on the basis that according to 2 Maccabees 2, **Jeremiah had hidden the Ark and the Altar in a hallow cave,** during and in the context of the Babylonian captivity, and consequently prophesied that after the re-gathering from the captivity, the **Ark would be found and returned to Jerusalem.** In *Luke, Chapter One,* we read where the angel appeared standing on the right side of the Altar of Incense, in the Temple at Jerusalem. If the Ark was not in the Second Temple, it was around somewhere close. if the Altar was found, the Ark was found. Jeremiah hid it for that purpose and said it would be found when Israel returned.

"I will fill this house with glory", saith the Lord of Hosts. The glory of this latter house shall be greater than of the former. The Hebrew word for "*glory*" here is *kabad*, which is the same Hebrew word used in *Exodus and Lev. 9:23,*for the **glory overshadowing the Ark of the Covenant.** During the November, 1989 visit, Gary and I were discussing a discovery he had made. A piece of structure, or cave, was broken off between the two caves at Qumran. **In symbolism this would be between the First and Second Temple.** That could be where **Jeremiah hid the Ark.**

THE ARK REMOVED

When they removed the Ark, they broke this part off. The Maccabees state, that Jeremiah took the Ark, the Tabernacle, and the Altar and climbed **upon Mount Nebo where Moses beheld the Heritage of God**. **The Heritage of God was the land of Israel.** Then Jeremiah turned thither, or toward that land, and saw a hallow cave. Therefore, the cave was not at Nebo as many have supposed, but rather due East of Nebo in Israel, in the Valley of Achor, at Qumran. The hallow cave indicates it was man made,or hallowed out.If the two cave area symbolizes the First and Second Temple as we believe, then the Ark, being temporarily housed between the two caves, indicates it was placed there by Jeremiah between the First and Second Temple periods, during the Babylonian captivity as it were. **The only way you can ever obtain complete archeological proof is to dig it up.** The Ark was later removed and taken back to Jerusalem where it remains to this day. Any other Ark may exist, but it is a copy. We know that the real Ark was placed by the Levites, under King Josiah's orders, in the Temple at Jerusalem, some several hundred years after Solomon and his sons, and therefore was not taken by them out of Israel. *2 Chron. 35:3.*

A SPECIAL BLESSING

On November 23rd, the eve of my departure to return to the United States, Gary Collett and I were in Tel Aviv. We went into a shop by the Great Synagogue of Tel Aviv, to purchase a Kippah.

There we became involved in a strange, unusual and yet phenomenal experience. Departing from the small shop, an elderly man followed us a few feet and called my name, "Mr. Carman."

We just kept walking. I could not believe I was hearing this because the man had no way of knowing my name and I had never seen him before! He cried out a second time, "Mr. Carman," and we continued walking.

Then he said, "Mr. Carman", the third time and I turned to hear him say something like, "I give you a special blessing."

As we walked on our way, Gary looked at me and said, "Did you hear that? How did he know your name?" I didn't know, as we hadn't even called each other by our first names while in the shop. After walking a few blocks, we decided we should go back and get his picture, as we had our cameras with us. When we returned, Gary said to the man, "You called his name three times. How did you do that?" **The gentleman just smiled, and pointed up to heaven.**

I have included this story because I do believe in miracles. I believe prophets will return to Israel in accordance with the Scriptures. I believe in the Bible prophecy of the End-time as related to Israel. And, I believe I am in the Will of God in working as I am, being led by the Spirit of God. *Rom. 8:14.* Therefore **to me, this was a sign of God's approval.**

One cannot just begin digging in Israel without proper authorization from the Israeli Government and without being approached by the Israeli Army.

The search for the Ashes of the Red Heifer, other Temple Treasures, and Scrolls is a continuing project with which I plan to be involved for as long as it takes through the 1990's. But, whether or not our team or I find these articles, they will be found **in God's Own Time.**

STRANGERS FROM A FAR COUNTRY

Chapter Twenty-One

The question is often asked, why are the Jewish people in Israel not expending more effort to locate and recover the Temple Treasures? Why do the Gentiles have to do this? God will not remind Israel to locate these treasures with the Ark of the Covenant. The **Jewish** people themselves have **a tradition that strangers will come from a far country to find their treasures** and help them restore their former desolations.

INTERNATIONAL CONFERENCE

In 1968, after recovering Jerusalem, Jews convened an International Conference in Jerusalem, to determine the next steps to take regarding the temple, since just the year before they had liberated the Temple Mount. They decided to do nothing, except submit to the ancient tradition of **waiting for the strangers.**

There are scriptures to support this position. Their Temple was left desolate in 70 AD, and their Tabernacle Vessels were hidden,or buried.

📖 **Matthew 23:36-38,** ³⁶*"Verily I say unto you, All these things shall come upon this generation.* ³⁷*0, Jerusalem, Jerusalem, thou that killest the prophets, and stonest them which are sent unto thee, how often would I have gathered thy children together, even as a hen gathereth her chickens under her wings, and ye would not!* ³⁸*Behold, your* **house is left unto you** *desolate."*

📖 **Isaiah 61:4-5,** ⁴*"And they shall build the old wastes,* **they shall raise up the former desolations,** *and they* shall **repair the waste cities**, *the desolations of many generations.* **5***And strangers shall stand and feed your flocks,* and the sons of the alien shall be your plowmen and your vine dressers.*"*

"Strangers", in Hebrew, is *Natzerim*, meaning **Sect of the Nazarenes.** *Acts 24:5,* "Nazarene", **separated or called out ones.** These were to raise up Israel's former desolations. *Isaiah 60:10,* strangers were to build up the walls of her cities. Beginning in *1 Kings 8:41*, **Solomon prayed for God to help the stranger that would come from a far country, to build the House, or Temple of the Lord.** The Gentiles would hear of the Lord's Name and serve Him. Some would even help rebuild, or repitch the Tabernacle of David, **because of the Lord's Name,** *Acts.15:14-17, Amos 9:11-12.* The Gentile Nations round about would know that the **God of Israel is God,** *Ezekiel 37:26-28.* God replied to Solomon that He would answer his prayer. **The *Natzerim* are the called out of the Gentiles for His Name.**

The Temple Mount of Israel must be cleansed with the Ashes of the Red Heifer in running water, before the Tabernacle can be set up again. *Ezekiel 36:22,23,25,*and *Numbers 19.*

"Strangers" therefore, **will come from a far country** to accomplish the finding of the Ashes of the last Red Heifer Sacrifice and the Tabernacle Treasures. These are preparations for the re-setting of the Tabernacle. I believe the "far country" is a country which has supported Israel in the past.

📖 **Gen. 12:2-3,** 2"And I will make of thee a great nation, and I will bless thee, and make thy name great; and thou shalt be a blessing: 3And **I will bless them that bless**

thee, and curse him that curseth thee: and in thee shall all families of the earth be blessed."
I believe the"far country" is a country which has been used of God and has a special destiny, to spread the Gospel of Jesus around the world. I believe the "far country" is a country that has served as a haven, for the gathering together of many nations,the down trodden, the poor exiles from bondage. **The United States** was the first country to recognize Israel as a nation-state, in 1948.

UNITED STATES CURRENCY

That "far country" is the United States of America, the only country outside Israel whose **currency bears the symbols of the Jewish Tabernacle.**

During the American Revolutionary War for Independence, beginning in 1776, the United States was in dire need of finances for the war. **A Jewish merchant** from Philadelphia, **Haym Salomon** was a major financier of the war, on behalf of the Continental Congress. He **donated his life's savings** and even **borrowed money for the effort.** Mr. Salomon was an Assistant to Robert Morris, Director of US. Finance during the war. Haym Salomon **died a pauper**. Refer to the Encyclopedia Britannica, and American Jewish Archives, 3101 Clifton Ave., Cincinnati, OH.

Haym Salomon was characterized by Robert Morris as "useful to the public interest," and James Madison called him, "our little friend in Front Street."

When the designs and symbols of the Dollar Bill were adopted by Congress, they were originated from the Middle East, and Israel in particular. (Department of the Treasury Bureau of Engraving and Printing, Washington, DC 20228) and (The Great Seal of the United States by Maury Maverick available at the Bureau of Engraving and Printing). The Dollar Bill is inscribed with the Latin Words, *"ordo novus seclurum,"* **meaning a new secular order of Gentiles.** The Hebrew equivalent of these words have the numerical value of *5537.* **On the Jewish calendar *5537* is *1776* on our calendar.** The birth year of the U.S.A. On the Dollar Bill is also *E. Pluribus Unum,* meaning, **out of many, one. Called out of many to be One.**

The Eagle is the symbol of the U.S.A. (Maury Maverick and the Bureau of Engraving). The U.S.A. has mounted up with wings of an eagle to help Israel. Most recently flying over Bozrah, *Jer. 49:22.* Between its wings, a box, the **Ark of the Covenant as between the wings** of the Cherubim, *Ex. 25.* **Above the eagle is the thirteen pillared cloud that led Israel through the wilderness. The cloud that was over the Holy of Holies** where the Ark rested. There are **thirteen arrows** held on one side by the eagle, and **thirteen olive branches** on the other side, **representing Justice and Mercy, or Peace.** There were **thirteen original colonies** of the U.S.A. There were also **thirteen tribes of Israel,** when two tribes emerged from Joseph. That is Ephraim and Manasseh, G*en, 48:14.*The thirteenth year is also the year of Bar Mitzvah in the life of a Jew. There are thirteen rows of stone in the pyramid. **The Menorah,** or Seven Golden Candlesticks, is under the Eagle, when the dollar bill is turned upside down. Then above the Seven Lamps, is the **Nine Feathered Tails,** which symbolizes the **Nine Flames of the Hanukkah Menorah.** The Hanukkah is related to the **Feast of the Dedication of the Temple,** in December, *St. John 10:22.*

There are 120 white spaces between the lines of the pyramid, **representing 120 Jubilees,** chronologically since Adam. Every 50th year was a Jubilee Year. Thus, 50 x

120, is 6,000 years from Adam. Across the second row on the right of the pyramid stones, in faint letters by a strong microscope is the word **Zion.**

The dollar is good as long as we "trust" in the God of Israel. The one true God. When the dollar collapses, a Jubilee Year will be proclaimed. The last one, and God's Glory will cover the earth. The All-seeing Eye, is the incomprehensible one, made comprehensible to us through Jesus Christ and His shed blood. This is the "Eye of Providence" who designed all of this and led our forefathers to America. (also in Maury Mavericks writings and the Bureau of Engraving, Washington, DC.) There is the Aura of the Shekinah, or Glory of God ,behind the Eye.

There are **Two Trees** on either side of the pyramid representing the **Tree of knowledge** and the **Tree of Life**. These two trees are in every Orthodox Old Jewish Synagogue.

Why did God select Gentiles, or Strangers, to find the lost Treasures? This is essential to give knowledgeable Christians dialogue with Israel and the Rabbis of Jerusalem, to explain the relevance of the Tabernacle and Vessels to the Jewish people,as related to the Messiah.

The second reason lends **greater leverage for witnessing to the entire Gentile world.** Those **witnessing to the Jewish people** must understand Hebrew culture, and use the right keys in dealing with the issues that block reconciliation between Christian and Jew. We see Jesus as the Lamb of Salvation, the Jews see their Messiah coming as the Lion of the Tribe of Judah. When they see His work as both, there is reconciliation, and the Lion lays down with the Lamb. Blessed be Jesus, Yeshua.

195

Some have said the Tabernacle and other symbols on the dollar bill are the symbols of a cult known as the "Illuminate." While this may be true, **no cult originated these symbols. They originated from God to Moses** in the <u>Bible,</u> *Ex. 25-40.*

Satan is a copycat. A counterfeiter only counterfeits from **The Real Thing. But the strangers have arrived, in this final Generation, for the raising of the Tabernacle.**

END-TIME REVIVAL HARVEST

Chapter Twenty-Two

The prophet Joel envisioned the land of Israel, lying as waste, swamps, and desolation, **followed by restoration.**

📖 **Joel 2:23-25,** *23"Be glad then, ye children of Zion, and rejoice in the Lord your God; for He hath given you the former rain moderately, and **He will cause** to come down for you the rain, **the former rain,** and the **latter rain in the first month.** 24And the floors shall be full of wheat, and the vats shall overflow with wine and oil. 25And **I will restore to you the years** that the locust hath eaten, the cankerworm, and the caterpillar, and the palmer worm, my great army which I sent among you."*

Afterward, there was to be a **universal outpouring of the Holy Spirit.**

📖 **Joel 2:28,** *"And it shall come to pass afterward, that **I will pour out my spirit upon all flesh;** and your sons and your daughters shall prophesy, your old men shall dream dreams, your young men shall see visions."*

Israel's land has been restored since 1948, and there has been a universal renewal of the Holy Spirit. I believe **the best is yet to come.**

THE GREAT AWAKENING

James refers to a **great outpouring of the Holy Spirit** and a great **harvest of souls** just **prior** to the **Return of Jesus** Christ.

📖 **James 5:7-8,** *7"Be patient therefore, brethren, unto the Coming of the Lord. Behold, the husbandman waiteth for the precious fruit of the earth, and hath long* *patience for it, **until he receive the early and latter rain.** ⁸Be ye **also patient; stablish your hearts:** for the Coming of the Lord draweth nigh."*

Notice this epistle was written to the scattered Twelve Tribes of Israel, *James 1:1.* **This Great End-time Revival-Harvest** has not yet reached its peak ,as of 1992. In fact, at present there is somewhat of a lull. **Before there can be a Great Harvest, there must be Great Revival, and before there can be Great Revival, there must be a "Great Awakening."** That awakening must **begin in the church.** God's people are the inner nucleus for God's relationship with the earth. They are the enlightened core, the salt of the earth. They **are the key that turns to God, to unlock healing in the land**.

📖 **2 Chron. 7:14,** *"If my people, which are called by my Name, shall **humble themselves,** and **pray,** and **seek my face,** and **turn** from their wicked ways; then will **I hear** from heaven, and will **forgive** their sin, and will **heal their land."***

The Great Awakening and Harvest is now beginning, as a result of catalysts already begun by the Persian Gulf Crisis. This tends to turn people's attention back to the Bible and focus their eyes on The Coming of the Lord. This is the most important thing, beyond controversial hair splitting doctrines, to **focus our attention on Jesus Christ and His Return.** A series of Mid-East Wars, and also positive events occurring in Israel, will accomplish a "stirring of hearts," and Great Harvest.

NOT SURVIVALISTS
BUT REVIVALISTS

Let us not be survivalists, but revivalists. The disciples of Jesus were instructed to impart unto the Gentiles, the Gospel of Salvation, through Jesus Christ, *Mark 16:14-15.* Again he said, "Follow me, and I will make you fishers of men." *Matt. 13:47,49,* [47] *"Again, the Kingdom of Heaven is like unto a net, that was cast into the sea, and gathered of every kind.* [49]*So shall it be at the end of the world; the angels shall come forth, and sever the wicked from among the just."* Here Jesus is comparing the Gospel to a net, in this case, cast into the Sea of Nations, and gathers of every nation, kindred and tongue. This was to occur at the end of the "*world*," in Greek, *aion* or *age.*

📖 **Matt. 24:14,** *"And this gospel of the **Kingdom shall be preached** in all the world **for a witness** unto all nations; and then shall the end come."*

WHAT WILL IT TAKE TO WAKE THEM

Time and again throughout history, when secularism has failed to solve the problems of society, man has turned to God, and spiritual revival emerged. We are approaching such a time now. There shall be distress of nations with perplexity, *Luke 21:25.* The word "*perplexity*" here, is derived from the Greek word *aporia,* **meaning no solution. No way out as far as man is concerned.** H.G. Wells, the famous Historian said, "For man and his world, there is no way out." Many times today we hear people remark, "People are asleep, **what will it take to wake them up, and stir the Christian community?** Something is going to have to happen." We will answer with a question. What has it always taken?

Various environmental conditions, man's failing efforts, despair and perplexity. Hearts seeking God. Major **changes in world affairs.** A conditioning process. The

proper season and mental, or emotional climate. A feeling of **remorse**, an atmosphere for Godly repentance. A feeling of **utter helplessness.** The season for harvest is summer. The season of Israel's restoration, The Budding Fig Tree, *Luke 21:29-31.*

POSITIVE AND NEGATIVE CATALYSTS

In this context, there will be a number of major catalysts to precipitate the next great **Revival Harvest.** There will be **negative catalysts** and **positive catalysts.** There will be negative catalysts such as the Aids disease, and a hundred other rare, mysterious diseases, the drug,alcohol problems, international terrorism and domestic violence, droughts, changes in weather patterns, upheavals, and a host of unsolvable problems along with wars and rumors of wars in the Middle East.

📖 **Matt. 24:1-8,** *[1]"And **Jesus** went out, and departed from the Temple: and his **disciples** came to Him for to show Him the buildings of the Temple. [2]And Jesus said unto them, **See ye not all these things?** Verily I say unto you, there shall not be left here one stone upon another, that shall not be thrown down. [3]And as he sat upon the Mount of Olives, the disciples came unto Him privately, saying, Tell us, when shall these things be? And what shall be the sign of thy coming, and of the end of the world? [4]And Jesus answered and said unto them, **Take heed that no man deceive you.** [5]For many shall come in My name, saying, I am Christ; and shall deceive many. [6]And ye **shall hear of wars and rumors of wars:** see that ye be not troubled; for all these things must come to pass, but **the end is not yet.** [7]For nation shall rise against nation, and kingdom against kingdom: and there shall be **famines, and pestilences,*** *and earthquakes, in diverse places.* [8] *All these are the beginning of sorrows.* "

GOD WILL BLESS AMERICA AGAIN

There will be **positive catalysts,** such as **The Great Hebrew Renaissance,** *Acts 15:14-17, Amos 9:11-15, Ezek.37:26-28, Ezek. 38:23, Joel 2;23-28, Ps. 102:15.* There will be the proclamation of God's Word, including Bible prophecy expostulation. **God will bless America again, through a warning message,** and by **giving space for repentance. With this will come revival** such as the world has never witnessed.

📖 **Matt. 24:14,** *"And this gospel of the Kingdom shall be preached in all the world for a witness unto all nations; and then shall the end come.* "

DECADE OF DESTINY

Salvation will be evidenced by a rainbow at midnight. *Ps. 98. Rev. 10.* The next decade. The decade of the 1990's will truly be a "**Decade of Destiny**" in every sense of the word. It will offer a **grand opportunity to spread the Gospel of Jesus Christ into every corner of the world.** It will give Christian people the opportunity to utilize Bible prophecy, Endtime events and signs, and the invigorating message of our Lord's Return, to win thousands for the Kingdom of God.

DECADE OF DISCOVERY

I believe the 1990's will also be a "**Decade of Discovery,**"a discovery of the hidden Treasures of the Jewish Temple,and the priceless Ark of the Covenant. Discovery of Biblical

Artifacts, giving credence to the validity of the <u>Holy Bible.</u> **Discovery of the effectiveness of the Holy Spirit to solve human problems.** The **discovery of deliverance by many people by the Power of God,** in Jesus Christ, throughout the world. **The unveiling of His Magnificence,** the accuracy of **His Prophetic Word**, and the promises of **His Divine Love.** I believe we will witness the **Greatest Spiritual Harvest in History.** This is the finest hour of the church. **Our greatest opportunity.** The doors are opening in nations formerly closed to the gospel. Already there is a cry in China for God and freedom. It is reported there are now 100 million Christians in China.

Tracts can be prepared to intensify and stimulate the message, gaining souls for Jesus. Before Jesus returns, mankind must be given every opportunity to receive Him into their hearts.

When Jesus comes at last, the cataracts of spiritual blindness shall be removed from the eyes of nations by the "Scalpel of Truth," and the Light of God's Glory shall shine from the Living Word "etched in their hearts", by the FLAMING FINGER OF GOD, Isa. 25:7.

AZURE JEWEL

The earth will be transformed into an Azure Jewel for 1,000 years, joining the symphony of the universe, singing praise unto the Almighty. Finally, the earth shall pass through the shadow of infinity and rest under the abode of that HOLY CITY, NEW JERUSALEM. Rev. 21.

There is a series of three major events to focus upon:

202

ONE : The Restoration of Israel. *Acts 1:6*

TWO: A Great End-time World Wide Harvest. *Acts 1:8*
THREE: The Return Of Jesus Christ. *Acts 1:11*

Thes are occurring one after the other **TO THE END**.
Matt. 24:14

THE KINGDOM OF GOD

Chapter Twenty-Three

The word *"Kingdom"* in the Greek is *bascilia,* which means the **Kings Court or the Kings Dominion.** There are basically **three Kingdoms,** referred to in the scriptures. First, the **Kingdom of Israel,** or God's Kingdom in Israel, *Ex. 19:5-6.*

THREE KINGDOMS

There is also the **Millennial Kingdom** Reign of Jesus Christ for a thousand years duration, and in between there is the **Spiritual Kingdom** within the saints of God for a period of two thousand years. The Millennial Kingdom , *Rev. 20:4, 2 Pet. 3:8,* and the 3rd day of *Hos. 6:2.* The Kingdom of the 2,000 year Church age , *Col. 1:13, Heb. 12:28, and Luke 17:21.* During those two days, or two thousand years, Jesus has continued to heal the sick, cast out devils and perform miracles, *Luke 13:32-33; Mark 16:19-20; Heb. 4:15.* By the 3rd day, His Body is perfected, complete,. and Jesus is still alive. He did not perish out of Jerusalem. Jesus spent two days with the Gentile Samaritans, indicating his two thousand year visit, or dwelling in the church among the Gentiles.

📖 **St. John 4:40,** *"So when the **Samaritans** were come unto him, they besought him that he would tarry with them: and **he abode there two days."***

📖 **Hos. 6:2,** *"After two days will he revive us: in the third day he will raise us up, and we shall live in his sight."*

📖 **St. John 7:33-35,** [33] *"Then said Jesus unto them, Yet a little while am I with you, and then I go unto him that sent me.* [34] *Ye shall seek me, and shall not find me: and where I am, thither ye cannot come.* [35] *Then said the Jews among themselves, Whither will he go, that we* *shall not find him? Will he go unto the dispersed,among the Gentiles, and teach the Gentiles?"*

St. John 13:36, "Simon Peter said unto him, Lord, whither goest thou? Jesus answered him, Whither I go, thou canst not follow me now; but thou shalt follow me afterwards." *Acts 10, Acts 15:14-16,* "Simeon hath declared how God at the first did visit the Gentiles, to take out of them **a people for His Name.** And to this agree the words of the prophets; as it is written, After this I will return, and will build again the Tabernacle of David, which is fallen down; and I will build again the ruins thereof, and I will set it up."

THE RAPTURE

There has been much recent discussion about The Rapture. Some say there is no Rapture because the word "Rapture" is not in the Bible. Some say it occurred in the early church, or in 70 AD and therefore has already been fulfilled. Some say the rapture will only serve as a welcoming committee for Jesus to return to earth. Some say Jesus will never even come back to earth. Some say He will return at the close of the Millennium. Some say the Millennium is not a literal thousand years, but is symbolic, beginning with Jesus obtaining victory over Satan, on the cross.

The words demon, trinity, grandfather, Millennium, theology, are not in the Bible, but the concept of these terms are indelible in the Scriptures. The Apostle Paul, *1 Thess. 4:16-17,* says, "**The Lord Himself** (personally, using the personal pronoun, the direct personal entity of Christ Jesus) **shall positively descend** , come down, from heaven (Greek *oranous*) with a shout (joyfully) with the voice of the archangel, and with the trump of God: and the dead in Christ shall rise first: Then we which are alive and remain shall be caught up,in Greek , *Harpadzo,* meaning **to be**

205

snatched away, ejected, or rapture, together with them in the clouds, to meet the Lord , (Personal Jesus,) **in the air, -** or atmosphere , and so shall we ever be with the Lord." Again Paul said, "I have a desire to depart, and to be with Christ," *Phil. 1:23.*

Phil. 3:20-21, "For our citizenship is in heaven, from which also we eagerly wait for a Savior, the **Lord Jesus Christ: "Who will transform the body of our humble state into conformity with the body of His Glory,** by the exertion of the power that He has even to subject all things to Himself." Paul is still placing this as a future event. *Tit. 2:13,* still future. *1 John 2:28,* still future. *1 Cor. 15:51-53,* still future. When will the event occur?

Many people in the church of Thessalonica were also thinking Jesus was returning in their day,after receiving Paul's first letter. Then the apostle writes a second letter of explanation. He writes,

📖 **2 Thess. 2:1-3,** *[1]"Now we request you, brethren, with regard to **the Coming of our Lord Jesus Christ,** and our gathering together to Him, [2]that you may not be quickly shaken from your composure, or be disturbed either by a spirit or a message or a letter as if from us, to the effect that the day of the Lord has come. [3]Let no one in any way deceive you, for **it will not come unless the apostasy comes first, and the man of lawlessness is revealed, the son of destruction."***

He is allocating the **Great Rendezvous or Gathering** in the air and the Return of Jesus to the Day of Christ,or the Day of the Lord, which every Bible scholar knows is the seventh day. The 7th day of the world week. **As that Day begins, the Rapture is fulfilled when the Lord returns for the** saints, and then at the close of the tribulation, he returns in glory with the saints,*1 Thess. 3:13, Jude 14, Rev. 19,* at the beginning of the seventh thousandth years.

This is why we are preparing for the **Greatest Airlift in History.** HAVE YOU PURCHASED YOUR TICKET YET? Your ticket is validated by the **blood of Christ Jesus,** and it is yours when you accept Jesus into your heart, believing he was raised from the dead. Then you are raised with Him to walk in newness of life, *Rom. 10:9, Rom. 6:4.*

THE LORD'S DAY

The Millennium Kingdom is a literal, thousand year reign of Jesus Christ and the Saints upon the earth, *Rev. 20:4; Rev. 5:9-10; Dan. 7:27; 2 Pet. 1:11; Zech.14:9,* **the Seventh Day, the Lord's Day.** *Gen. 2:3,* six days, or six thousand years allotted to man, the seventh is the Lord's Day. **A Rest from man's rule,** whose breath is in his nostrils, *Ex. 20, Isa. 2:22.*

The first six days were six literal thousand years from Adam, were they not? *Gen. 5:1-3.* Likewise the seventh is a thousand years. The Lord Returns at the close of two days, or **2,000 years,** thus, at the beginning of the third thousandth day **from his birth on earth,** *2 Pet 3:8, Ps. 90:4, Hos. 6:2-3,* "After two days will he revive us: in the third day he will raise us up, and we shall live in his sight. Then shall we know, if we follow on to know the Lord; his going forth is prepared as the morning; and he shall come unto us as the rain, as the latter and former rain unto the earth." He returns soon after the restitution of all things pertaining to the Kingdom of Israel, *Acts 3:20-21.* He returns in Glory in the **same generation** of Israel's restoration,. Ps. 102:13-18, Luke 21:24-32,

📖 **Matt. 24:30,** *"And then shall appear the **sign of the Son of man in heaven:** and then shall all the tribes of the earth mourn, and **they shall see the Son of man coming in the clouds** of heaven with power and great glory."*

He Returns with the Saints in Glory at the close of the tribulation period, or 70th week of Daniel, *Dan. 9:27; Matt. 24:29-30; Rev. 13:17-19.* He destroys the anti-Christ on the Mount of Olives, and that closes the anti-Christ of final 3½ years, *Rev. 13:5,7, 2 Thess. 2:8.*

📖 **Zech. 14:12,** *"and this shall be the **plague** wherewith the Lord **will smite all the people that have fought against Jerusalem**;Their flesh shall consume away while they stand upon their feet, and their eyes shall consume away in their holes,and their tongue shall consume away in their mouth."*

He then commences the resplendent Golden Reign of the Millennial Kingdom. Jesus comes for the saints, at which time they put on immortality.

📖 **1 Cor. 15:52-53,** [52]*"In a moment, in the twinkling of an eye, at the last trump: for the trumpet shall sound, and the dead shall be raised incorruptible, and we shall be changed.* [53]*For this corruptible must put on incorruption, and this mortal must put on immortality."*

Phil. 3:20-21, **He then comes back** with the saints at the close of the Tribulation, and reigns in the **Father's Kingdom until even death dies.** *Matt. 24:29-30,*

"Immediately after the tribulation of those days shall the sun be darkened, and the moon shall not give her light, and the stars shall fall from heaven, and the powers of the heavens shall be shaken: And then shall appear the sign of the Son of man in heaven: and then shall all the tribes of the earth mourn, and they shall see the Son of man coming in the clouds of heaven with power and great glory" Then He turns the Kingdom back to the Father.

📖 **1 Cor. 15:23-28,** 23*"But every man in his own order; Christ the first fruits; afterward they that are Christ's at **His Coming.** 24Then cometh the end, when **He shall have delivered up the Kingdom to God, even the Father;** when he shall have put down all rule and all authority and power. 25For he must reign, till he hath put all enemies under his feet. 26**The last enemy that shall be destroyed is death.** 27For he hath put all things under his feet. But when he saith all things are put under him, it is manifest that he is excepted, which did put all things under him. 28And when all things shall be subdued unto him, then shall the Son also himself be subject unto him that put all things under him, that **God may be all in all.**"*

📖 **Matt. 26:29,** *"But I say unto you, I will not drink henceforth of this fruit of the vine, until that day when I drink it new with you in my Father's Kingdom."*

📖 **Rev. 20:1-4,** 1*"And I saw an **angel** come down **from heaven,** having the key of the bottomless pit and a great chain in his hand. 2And he **laid hold on the dragon, that old serpent,** which is the Devil, and Satan, and **bound him a thousand years,** 3And cast him into the bottomless pit, and shut him up, and **set a seal upon him, that he should deceive the nations no more,** till*

209

the thousand years should be fulfilled: and after that he must be loosed a little season. *4And I saw thrones, and they sat upon them, and judgment was given unto them: and I saw the **souls of them that were beheaded for the witness of Jesus**, and for the word of God, and which had not worshipped the beast, neither his image, neither had received his mark upon their foreheads, or in their hands; and **they lived and reigned with Christ a thousand years."**

THE GREAT TRIBULATION

Chapter Twenty-Four

What is the timing of the Great Tribulation portrayed in *Matt. 24:21*? Did it occur in the Generation of 70 AD. over 1,900 years ago, when Rome destroyed Jerusalem, or is it yet to come?

First of all, we must realize that **Jesus depicted the Great Tribulation in the Olivet Discourse,** just prior to his crucifixion. *Matthew, Mark* and *Luke* give parallel accounts, but different details of the discourse. We must then ask the question, **was the gospel preached to the entire habitable earth prior to 70 AD., *Matt. 24:14*?** Did **the abomination of desolation** in *verse 15*, occur prior to 70 AD.? This is a definite **no.**

Jesus is quoting from *Dan. 9:27*, regarding the **anti-Christ entering and defiling the Temple** in the middle of the seven year week. This did not occur in the generation of A.D.70. From *Rev. 4:1* on, was a vision of future events beyond John's time. *Rev. 13:5,* and *7,* involves the abomination of desolation, the rule of anti-Christ and the final 3½ years.

During the first 3½ years of the 7 years, the **two witnesses testify**, *Rev. 11:3*. During the last 3½ years of the seven year week, the anti-Christ defiles the Temple, or Holy Place, *Rev. 11:2 and 7.*

The abomination of desolation by anti-Christ in the Temple abounds for 3½ years until the Return of Jesus as Victor, *2 Thess. 2:4, 8.* There must be a Holy Place for the anti-Christ to stand in. Therefore, **the Holy Place will be restored, prior to the anti-Christ.** Again, Daniel depicts the anti-Christ expiring at the end of that last 3½ years of the seven year week, *Dan. 7:25-27. Matt. 24*, is written primarily to the **Jewish people,** who are to **flee to the**

211

Judean mountains and the wilderness, at that time. Again, this is during the final 3½years, or 1,260 days of the anti-Christ oppression , *Rev. 12:6*. This is all still future, *verse 20* again gives credence that *Matt. 24*, is speaking to Israel, in reference to the Sabbath day or *habot*.

📖 **Matt. 24:21,** *" For then shall be **Great Tribulation,** such as was not since the beginning of the world to this time, no, nor ever shall be."*

This is characterized as a tribulation unprecedented in world history. In 70 AD,according to Josephus' History of Jewish Wars, approximately 1 million, 100 thousand Jews were slaughtered in Israel as blood was spilled across Jerusalem and the Temple Mount. Thousands of Jews were crucified and others were taken captive as slaves by the Romans. From 1938-1945, there was a greater tribulation, when six million Jews perished from the face of the earth, in gas chambers and concentration camps in Germany and throughout Eastern Europe, under the Genocide, Jewish extermination conspiracy,of Adolf Hitler. This undoubtedly was more severe and of a greater magnitude than the terrible devastation of 70 AD.**Out of the ashes of the holocaust, arose Israel as a reborn nation, alive and well.** Therefore,in view of these facts, the greatest tribulation in world history did not occur in 70 AD. This is still a future event occurring under the auspices of anti-Christ, *Rev. 13, Rev. 6:2*.

The tribulation will be consummated at Armageddon, and the Return of Jesus Christ, with judgment upon the nations, *Rev. 11:15,18, Rev. 19:19-20, Rev. 20:1-3*. This shall be open judgment before the world, *Matt. 24:27-28*. For where ever the carcass, or dead are, the armies are gathered. **Jesus will Return at the End of the Tribulation, to Earth.** 📖 **Matt. 24:29-30**, [29]" *Immediately after the **tribulation** of those days shall the **sun be darkened**, and the **moon shall not give her light**, and the **stars shall fall** from heaven, and the **powers of the heavens shall be shaken:** [30]And then shall appear the **sign of the Son of man in heaven:** and then shall all the tribes of the earth mourn, and **they shall see the Son of man coming in the clouds of heaven with power and great glory.** "*

We ,the saints, were already caught up unto Him in the air. Then His feet never touched the earth, *ech.14:4.* *"Many shall come from the east and west, and shall sit down with Abraham,, and Isaac, and Jacob, in the **Kingdom of Heaven.**" Matt. 8:11, Zech. 14:16, Luke 13:28-29.*

Certainly John's experience on the Isle of Patmos transpired after 70AD. In fact some 25 years later, according to most scholars. *John* is still speaking of things to come thereafter.

Luke speaks of "the trodding down of Jerusalem until the Times of the Gentiles are fulfilled," which, in turn, would not be until the feet and ten toes of Nebuchadnezzar's historical Gentile image, and anti-Christ, *Dan. 2:43, Dan. chapter 7,* and *Dan. 9:24-27.* **Thus, we have cycled back again to the theme of the final 3½ years of The Holy Place Abomination and Tribulation,described in *Matt. 24:15-22.***

WELCOME TO THE KINGDOM AGE

Chapter Twenty-Five

"Having **marched** through the harvest fields with Gospel Sickles in our hands, having surveyed God's army passing over the plains, mountains, and through the spring fed valleys of the land, we have seen the Rapture, looked with astonishment at wars, revolutions, and famines.We **viewed** the mysterious signs of the heavens, **heard** the rumbling of earthquakes, and the reeling earth beneath and finally with man's arms full of weapons, we **witnessed** the approaching armies of the world enter the field of combat for Armageddon. **It is done**," *Rev. 16:16-17.*

Then **we see the new day light break forth** full and fair, as Jesus returns to judge the nations and to establish His Righteous Kingdom. **Welcome to the Kingdom.** *Rev. 19:11, Matt. 13:43, Prov. 4:18.*

British Editor Malcolm Muggeridge says, "It has become abundantly clear in the second half of the Twentieth Century that **Western man has decided to abolish himself**. Having wearied of the struggle to be himself, he has created his own boredom out of his own affluence, his own impotence out of his own erotimania, his vulnerability out of his own strength, himself blowing the trumpet that brings the walls of his own city tumbling down, until at last having **educated himself into imbecility** and polluted and drugged himself into stupefaction, he kneels over, a weary, battered old Tyrannosaurus and **becomes extinct.**"

Oh, but **there is a hope and a faith** beyond this dismal end of the age **for those who have been born again and follow His Word,** which is a lamp unto our feet and a light unto our pathway, *Ps. 119:105.*

OF THE MILLENNIUM BUT NOT YET IN IT

Welcome to the Kingdom Age. "Faith is the substance of the things hope for, the evidence of things not seen," *Heb. 11:1.* **Those who have the Word burning in their hearts,** already have within them the substance of the Millennial Age. **They are in the old world, but not of it, they are of the millennium, but not yet in it.** I see a world of love adorned with peace, a world in which no exile signs, no prisoner mourns, and where labor reaps its full reward.

I see a world. I see a world without the beggar's outstretched palm, without the piteous wail of want, the livid lips of lies, or the cruel eye of scorn. I see a world and as I look, life lengthens, peace abides, love grows, and all is united under the Eternal Star of Truth, Jesus the Christ.

Jesus will be victorious and triumphant. Those that are with him are called, chosen, and faithful because they are full of faith, *Rev. 17:14, Rom.10:17.* These are they who will truly **bind the earth with the Twine of Truth and the Loveliness of Love. Welcome to the Kingdom.**

CALL UPON THE NAME OF THE LORD

If you don't know this wonderful Savior, and **you are fearful** of this age and the things to come, and you want to escape the horrible things coming upon the earth, call upon Him and He will hear. For He says, **whosoever shall call upon the Name of the Lord shall be saved.** Jesus said, "watch ye therefore, and pray always, that ye may be accounted worthy to escape all these things that shall come to pass, and to stand before the Son of Man," *Luke 21:36.*

The **wonderful promise** to the Children of God, who are joint-heirs with Christ Jesus is, *Rom. 8:16-17.* "My **God**

215

shall supply all your needs according to His riches in Glory by Christ Jesus," *Phil. 4:19.* Welcome to the Kingdom Age.

NEW EARTH RECHARGED

During the Kingdom Age, streams will be purified, rivers cleared, the air freshened, the earth recharged, a slightly thicker atmosphere, a more even global temperature will prevail upon the earth. The soil will become more fertile, new crops and fruits will grow,

📖 **Rom. 8:19-22,** [19]*"For the **earnest expectation** of the creature waited for the manifestation of the Sons of God.* [20]*For the creature was made subject to vanity, not willingly, but by reason of him who hath subjected the same in hope.* [21]*Because **the creature itself also shall be delivered from the bondage of corruption into the glorious liberty of the children of God.*** [22]*For we know that the whole creation groaneth and travaileth in pain together until now."*

Trees will begin to bear fruit that do not now bear fruit. **The presence and glory of God will charge the very air around the earth,** *Ps. 72:19.* **The life span** of hundreds of thousands **will increase.**① The **earth will flourish, Love will govern, Justice will prevail and Peace will arise as a song upon the breezes of the air.** The symphonies of praise and thanksgiving to God will ring out everywhere. **The first dominion will be restored to those in Christ Jesus, the second man Adam,** *Gen.1:28, Micah 4:8, Ps. 8:4-8.* The heavenly **order of the Nations will arise** like a beautiful dream. The deserts will blossom and springs will emerge from nowhere. The hidden riches of the earth will bud forth to meet the human race.Jesus Christ shall truly ring in this **Golden Age** of a thousand years, until it **prepares a Kingdom Remnant** from the Nations that will unite with eternity and endless bliss. All the rivers of gladness and joy, all the aspirations of the human soul, all the dreams of men, women and nations, all the gifts and powers of God ,with the rich and endless depths of his benevolent love, **all shall flow as a river into the Great Ocean of Eternity** where the **Saints** of God **shall abide.**

Satan shall be loosed a little season, but notice Satan and his forces are swallowed up in fire and annihilated, *Rev. 20:9, Isa. 2:22.* The saints shall live and rejoice in the indescribable wonders of the creator's ecstasy. Jesus Christ will have begun **His Resplendent Reign** and the sentiments of John Greenleaf Whittier will have truly been fulfilled as a beautiful dream resurrected upon the earth. *"Drop thy still dews of quietness till all our strivings cease; take from our soul the strain and stress, and let our ordered lives confess, the beauty of thy peace. Breathe, thy coolness and thy balm, let sense be dumb, let flesh retire, speak through the earthquake, wind, and fire. O still small voice of calm."*

Welcome to the Kingdom.

WHY I DO NOT ACCEPT
THE "KINGDOM NOW" DOCTRINE

Chapter Twenty-Six

This is a rather elusive subject. If you are referring to the **Spiritual Kingdom as being now,** to this **I AGREE.** We have always known that. *Col. 1:13,* "Who hath delivered us from the power of darkness, and hath translated us into the Kingdom of His Dear Son:"

📖 **Heb. 12:28,***"Wherefore, receiving a kingdom which cannot be moved, let us have grace, whereby we may serve God acceptably with reverence and godly fear."*

📖 **Rom. 14:17,** *"For the **Kingdom of God** is not meat and drink; but **Righteousness, and Peace, and Joy in the Holy Ghost."***

If you say, **God's people** are "**now**" the **SEED of the millennial Kingdom,** and are **preparing** or **warning** the nations relative to the return of Jesus Christ, **I CAN AND DO,AGREE.**

If you say,the **body of Christ** is God's millennial **Kingdom** people, or **officiating body** of government or a **Kingdom in exile** as it were, **I AGREE.**

📖 **Luke 19:12-13, 17-19,** [12]*"He said therefore, A certain nobleman went into a far country to **receive for himself a kingdom, and to return.** [13]And he called his ten servants, and delivered them ten pounds, and said unto them, **Occupy 'til I come.** [17]And he said unto him, Well, thou good servant: because thou hast been faithful in a very little, have thou authority over ten cities. [18]And the second came, saying, Lord, thy pound* *hath gained five pounds.* *19And he said likewise to him, Be thou also over five cities."*

If you say, the **basic principles** of the **Kingdom Age** are to be incorporated **into our individual lives now, and** in the life and teachings **of the church** as a collective entity, **I AGREE**, and it is all **fulfilled in Love.** Jesus taught us to love one another , *1 Pet. 2:24 and St. John 13:34.*

The people of God are "of" the millennial kingdom, but not yet "in" it, they are "in" the world, but not "of" it.

📖 **Hebrews 11:1,** *"Now **faith** is the substance of the things **hoped for,** the evidence **of things not seen.** "*

The substance, or essence, of the Millennial Kingdom, dwells within our hearts now, Jesus said,

📖 **Luke 17:21,** *"The Kingdom of God is within you."*

The Greek word for "**kingdom**", is *bascilia,* or the **king's court, the kingdom, or dominion.** Thus, the King's court or dominion is **within you.**

📖 **Col. 1:27,** *"Christ in you the hope of glory."*

The substance of the fruit is in the seed, even before the fruit develops visibly. **If you are saying, the actual Millennial Kingdom is now in existence and functioning, I STRONGLY DISAGREE.**

If you are saying,that we ourselves, as the church, are going to bring into existence and produce the Millennial Kingdom, prior to the return of Jesus Christ to this earth, **I WILL UNEQUIVOCALLY AND VERY PERSISTENTLY, DISAGREE WITH YOU.**

219

First of all, the Millennial Kingdom Age involves the assimilation and absorption of the kingdoms of this world into the Kingdom of our Lord, *Rev. 11:15.* This, by any stretch of the imagination, has not happened.

Satan will be bound for one thousand years, *Rev. 20:1-4.* That simply has not happened. If the Devil is bound now in our world, I would surely dread to see him loose! If the Lord has chained him now, he certainly has him on a very long leash!

There are a number of prophetic fulfillment's to occur before the return of Christ , not necessarily before the Rapture. For example, the Tabernacle of David will be recovered and restored in Jerusalem, *Amos 9:11-14; Matt. 24:15; Rev. 11:1-3.*

There are **several impediments** between now and the tangible realization of the Millennial Kingdom Age. A major impediment is the emergence of the anti-Christ, *Dan. 9:27.* In fact, the Scriptures are lucid and precise in the timing on this matter. *Rev.11:2,3 and 7,* portrays the **development of the Tabernacle, and the anti-Christ prior to the Kingdom Age,** in *Rev. 11:15.* The full rage of anti-Christ is in fact a pre-requisite for the return of Christ Jesus to earth and the execution of His power and authority to obliterate the anti-Christ.

The church, or no other power on earth will be able to accomplish the annihilation of the anti-Christ.

📖 **2 Thess.2:7-8,** [7]*"For the mystery of iniquity doth already work: only **he who now hinders** will hinder, until he be **taken out of the way.** *[8]*And then shall that*

> *wicked be revealed, whom* **the Lord shall consume** *with the spirit of his mouth, and shall destroy with the brightness of his coming."*

Once the church, or restrainer, is caught away , the anti-Christ will rule, *2 Thess. 2:6,7.*

The mere expectation and the promulgation of **teachings** for transforming the world into the **Kingdom Age, prior to the Return of Jesus Christ,** can engender **a form of humanism,** tantamount to Satan's first lie, "you shall be as Gods," *Gen. 3:5.*

Our efforts will not **result** in the establishment of a functioning millennium. This would be the generation and **inception of the Kingdom without the King.**

These teachings, penetrating the minds of many, that we are going to bring into being the Millennium Kingdom *"on earth now",* **could contribute to the power base of that very anti-Christ with the rudiments of new ageism, humanism, and humanistic one worldism.**

WE NEED TO CENTER OUR ATTENTION
ON **CHRIST IN US** THE HOPE OF GLORY,
NOT ON THE IDEA THAT WE CAN EFFECT
THE TIMING OF HIS RETURN.

221

SCENARIO OF EVENTS

Chapter Twenty-Seven

As prophetic events are fulfilled, Bible Prophecy interest among the public will naturally increase. The 1990's will not only be the last decade of the 20th Century, but it will also be the last decade of a two thousand year period since the birth of Jesus, and the last ten years of a 6,000 year period. **These are truly momentous times.**

Our vision as **Christians must transcend** the present height of this age, to behold the wonders of the Kingdom Age. Yet we must also **stand up** for what is right in our present age, with vision and conviction. We should always **witness** to mankind and even to leaders of our nation as to what should be in accordance with God's word, especially concerning moral and social issues. The Bible itself is a compendium of men and women of God, speaking forth their convictions in their respective nation or culture. **We have an obligation to warn,** to **witness** and to **propagate God's Word,** in the spirit of love and concern. We have a mandate from the heavenly throne to **proclaim God's Word in love and to manifest charity** with regard to humanitarian endeavors, *Acts1:8, Ezek.33:7-9, 2 Tim. 4:2.*

We have not heard the last cry for democracy and freedom in China. A Pan-European alliance is being formed between East and West Europe. The erection of the Berlin Wall symbolized the dividing of nations, the crumbling of the Berlin Wall signifies the uniting of nations into a world order. Germany will eventually become neutralist, as will Europe. A series of Arab - Mideast Wars have been fused, as viewed in a panoramic vision by Isaiah, Jeremiah and Ezekiel, some 2500 - 2700 years ago, in advance, as portrayed in Chapter 9. I fully expect the recovery of The Kalil treasure and the other Temple Vessels in the midst of all this, as spotlighted in *Ezek. 37:26-28 and Amos 9:11.* I believe all of this will generate **A Great Harvest** in the 1990's, *Joel 2:25-28.* **Merkoveh Chariots of Fire will hover over the Earth** , *Joel 2:28-31, Isa. 66:15.*

The Cloud of Glory will cover Old Jerusalem as in days of old, *Amos 9:11, Lev.9:23.*The **144,000 Jewish witnesses** will be turned loose, *Rev. 7.* **Elijah will return, the two Witnesses on the scene,** *Mal. 4:5, Rev. 11.*

The Rapture will occur at any time, date undisclosed. The anti-Christ will emerge while a temporary peace is brought forth.During this time, Magog invades Israel and is defeated, *Dan. 8:25, Ezek. 38:11.* The anti-Christ enters the Tabernacle, the Holy Place , *Matt. 24:15, Dan. 9:27, and 2 Thess. 2.* The last seven plagues are poured out, *Rev. 15-16.* The Great Tribulation and wrath follow. The Raptured Saints are not here, *1 Thess. 5:9.*

Then, **Armageddon** develops with the anti-Christ and his forces from the West, and nations from the East converging upon Israel, to fight a holy war and to solidify their power over Jerusalem. **This is a collision between East and West.**

📖 **Rev. 16:12-16,** 12*"And the sixth angel poured out his vial upon the great river Euphrates; and the water thereof was dried up, that the way of the kings of the east might be prepared. *13*And I saw three unclean spirits like frogs come out of the mouth of the dragon, and out of the mouth of the beast, and out of the mouth of the false prophet. *14*For they are the spirits of devils, working miracles, which go forth unto the kings of the earth and of the whole world, to gather them to the battle of that great day of God Almighty. *15*Behold, I come as a thief. Blessed is he that* *watcheth, and keepeth his garments, lest he walk naked, ¹⁶and they see his shame. And he gathered them together into a place called, in the Hebrew tongue, Armageddon."*

Jesus Christ, Messiah, The King of Kings, will return, intervene in Armageddon, destroy the anti-Christ and the opposing forces of Jerusalem, *2 Thess. 2:8, Zech. 14:12.* Jesus Christ will then reign over the Earth as King of Kings, *Zech. 14:9,* His Headquarters will be in Jerusalem. *Jer. 3:17,* "At that time they shall call Jerusalem the Throne of the Lord; and all the nations shall be gathered unto it, to the name of the Lord, to Jerusalem: neither shall they walk any more after the imagination of their evil heart," *Ps. 76:2 and Zech. 14.* King David will resurrect and will be King of Jerusalem, under Jesus Christ, who will be King of Kings, *Rev. 19:13-16. Jer. 30:9,* "But they shall serve the Lord their God, and David their King, whom I will raise up unto them." *Ezek. 37:24,* "And David, My servant, shall be king over them; and they all shall have one shepherd: they shall also walk in My Judgments, and observe My Statutes, and do them."

SUMMARY OF MAJOR SIGNS FOR MESSIAH'S COMING.

Ψ   Restoration of Israel 5708 - 1948. Ezek. 37.

Ψ   Restoration of Jerusalem 5728 - 1967. Luke 21:24-32; Rom. 11; Isa. 61:4; Hos. 3:4-5; Ps. 71:22.

Ψ   Search for the Tabernacle Treasures . 1980's and 90's

Ψ   The search for Messiah in Israel . 1980 - 1990's. Matt. 23:37-39.

Ψ   The rebuilding of David's Harp. 1988

Ψ   The release of the Russian Jews . Isa. 43:6. 178,000
     in 1990.

Ψ   The cry of peace and safety movement toward a
     united Europe, a one world financial system, a one
     world political system, and a one world religious
     system.Rev.13:2,Rev.18:3,11;Dan.11:2124,28,31,36

Ψ   The time element, nearing the close of 2,000 years
     since the birth of Christ Jesus . Hos. 5:15 - 6:3.

Ψ   The blossoming of the Valley of Achor and the
     Judean Desert . Isa. 35:1, Hos. 2:15.

Ψ   International Upheaval and all Seven Olivet Major
     signs occurring at the same time and more
     frequently. Luke 21:8-11, and these contemporary
     with the Generation of Israel's restoration.

Ψ   The approaching 70th Jubilee of Israel coinciding
     with the restitution of all things pertaining to the
     Kingdom of Israel. Acts 1:6, Acts 3:20-21, Lev. 25.

Ψ   Ob. 4 - Space age and the increase of knowledge
     and technology . Dan. 12:4.

Ψ   Mid-East wars. Isa.23, Zech.11:1, Isa.13:4-6,14:24-
     27, Isa.31:5,8, Mi. 5:2-6, Isa. 17:1, Jer. 49:23-27,
     Jer. 49:1-4.

Ψ   The Magog invasion of Israel.   Ezek. 38-39,
     Armageddon. Rev.15,Rev.6:12-16; Dan. 11:31-45;
     Joel 3; Zech. 14:3-4.

Ψ International terrorism . Gen. 6:11, Luke 17:26-30.

Ψ Drugs and Satan worship . Rev. 9:21.

Ψ Signs in the heavens. Luke 21:11.

Ψ The Emerging Kings of the East . Rev. 16:12.

Ψ The Russian alliance with Arab States opposed to Israel. Ezek. 38:5 and many others.

Ψ The drying up of the Euphrates River. Rev. 16:12.

Ψ Arab axis of nations with aim of preventing Israel from being a nation . Ps. 83.

BIBLIOGRAPHY

Chapter One

(1)The word Zion in Hebrew can also be Tsee, Yone or Tsiyown.

(2)Confirmed in the Hebrew Dictionary of Strongs Concordance "Generation to Come" in Ps. 102:18. The Hebrew Dictionary. 1st ed. p. 30, ref.# 1755. p.11, ref. # 314.

(3)The restoration of Israel to their ancient land boundaries was depicted in Ezek. 37.

(4)Israel as the fig tree in Luke 21:29 is supported by many Bible Scholars. Dr. M.R. De Hoan, The Jew and Palestine in Prophecy. p. 168 & 176, chapters 22 & 23. J.Dwight Pentecost, Prophecy for Today, p. 222, chapter 17.

(5)Dr. Ams A. Shorrosh, an arab Christian raised in Nazareth in his book, Jesus Prophecy and the Middle East. H.L. Willmington, Signs of the Times. p. 131, chapter 21. Israel restored as the sign of the 2nd Coming is supported also by Dr. John F. Walnoord,Am.,ThD.,D.D. of Dallas Theological seminary.

(6)This position on the generation is supported by many Bible Scholars including Hal Lindsey, Countdown to Armageddon. Wilbur Smith,The Israeli - Arab Conflict.

Chapter Two

(1)1 Chron. 29:26-28. 2 Chron. 9:22,30.

(2)William L.Hull, The Fall and Rise of Israel.(Zondervan Pub. Co., 1954) p. 126, chapter 6.

(3)William L. Hull, The <u>Rise and Fall of Israel</u>. p.137-140.

Chapter Three

(1)Josephus History and Roman History.

(2)On the edge of the coin is inscribed the Hebrew letters GDDL: G = 3, D = 4, D = 4, L = 30 G= 3 , DD = 4-4 or 8, L = 30 Thus 3830. The year 3830 or 70 AD This is the year the destruction of Jerusalem occurred.

(3)Jesus and the disciples spoke Hebrew. It was the common language of their day. Oneal Carman, <u>GOLDEN AGE 2000</u> chap 7 complete Thesis providing evidence that Jesus spoke Hebrew.

Chapter Four

(1)Flavius Josephus,<u>History of Jewish Wars</u>.p.427

Chapter Eight

(1)Oneal Carman, <u>The Golden Age 2000</u> chap.7 Evidence that the great tribulation is at the close of the two thousand year period and not A.D. 70.
(2)Dr. John Wolnoord, <u>Prophecy of the Nations</u>.

Chapter Nine

(1)Professor Barry Fell, <u>American B.C</u>. - Dr. W.S. McBirine, <u>World War III and the United States</u>.

Chapter Fourteen

(2)James H. Charlesworth, Jesus Within Judaism. chapter 3,4,and 5. Shaye J.D. Cohen, From the Moccabees to the Mishnah. (Westminister Press, Philadelphia, Penn.)
(3)Copper scroll excerpts from the Translation of the Copper Scroll, John Allegro.
(4)Rabbi Maimonides, 12th century Jewish Rabbi, The Book of Numbers in the Jewish Midrash and The Mishnah..

(5)The Book of Numbers in The Jewish Midrash- Rabbi Maimonides, The Mishna Torah . Flavius Josephus, The Complete Works of Josephus. The Copper Scroll. The Jewish Halakhah. Holy Bible , Num. 19th chapter. (King James Version).

(6)Shaye J.D. Cohen, From the Maccabees to the Mishnah p-153, 156, 161, chapter 5. Geza Vermes Dead Sea Scrolls in English.

(7)Theodore H. Goster, Dead Sea Scriptures.(Garden City Doubleday and Co., 1976). Nathan Ansubel,The Book of Jewish Knowledge Encyclopedia - The Damascus Document. The Complete Works of Josephus . book 18, chapter 1, p. 377., book 2, chapter 8. Eerdman's Handbook of the Bible. Leon J. Wood, Professor of Old Testament, A Survey of Israels History . Studies and dean of the Grand Rapids Baptist Seminars.

(8)Joachin Jeremias, Jerusalem in the Time of Jesus (Fortress Press, Philadelphia, Penn.)

(9)The Mishna and the Midrash, The Book of Numbers.

(10)Meir Ben-Dov, and Mordechai Naor Zelv Aner, The Western Wall. (Pub. by Israeli Ministry of Defense, Publishing House, 1983, Jerusalem). p. 89-90, chapter 4.

(10)Meir Ben-Dov, and Mordechai Naor Zelv Aner, <u>The Western Wall.</u> (Pub. by Israeli Ministry of Defense, Publishing House, 1983, Jerusalem). p. 89-90, chapter 4.

Chapter Fifteen

(1)Temple of Solomon - 1, Temple - 2, Temple - 3 (Tabernacle of David or Tribulation) Ezekiels Temple - 4. <u>Holy Bible</u>, 2 Chron- 5. Book of Ezra. Amos 9:11. 2 Thess. 2:1-4. Ezek. 40-44.

Chapter Sixteen

(1)Dr. David A. Lewis, In <u>Prophecy 2000</u>. p. 152-158.

Chapter Twenty

(1)<u>Copper scroll,,GOLDEN AGE 2000</u>, ref chap 7.

Chapter Twenty-Two

(1)Hebrew Language, <u>GOLDEN AGE 2000</u>, ref. chap 7. .

Chapter Twenty-Five

(1)<u>Holy Bible</u>, Isa. 65:17-22, Isa- 2:2-4, Gen. 1:26-28, Mich 4:8, Rev. 20:4, 1 Cor- 15:23, Isa- 35:1, Hag. 2:7.